BELIEVE IT!

BELIEVE IT!

Randy Lang

VITALITY PUBLISHING LLC

Believe It! Randy Lang

Published by
Vitality Publishing, LLC

Book design by Eden Graphics, Inc.
www.edengraphics.net

Library of Congress Control Number: 2015905368
ISBN: 978-1-60645-135-9

10 9 8 7 6 5 4 3 2 1
First Printing
PRINTED IN THE UNITED STATES OF AMERICA

To my parents

CONTENTS

INTRODUCTION

I'M NOT SURE what age it is when you realize that you don't have the same stuff or the same quality of stuff as other kids. Clothes, shoes, baseball mitts, and bicycles: these are all the things kids notice. As this realization hits, a kid goes through a process. Some simply accept that others have better things and choose to be happy with what they have. Others have a desire to have nicer things, be it a pair of shoes or a new baseball mitt. I'm guessing that you've picked up this book because, like me, like most people, you're the latter type. I believe that most of us are able to see a gap between what we have or where we are and what we want or where we want to be, and that ignites a natural desire within us. The problem is, we don't all have a natural belief that we can achieve that desire on our own, or at all.

When you were a kid and you saw a friend or neighbor with something you wanted, you probably went to your parents or guardian to ask for it.

Maybe your father said, "Just be happy for what you have. Some people have nothing at all."

Maybe your mother said, "It's too expensive—we can't afford it."

I was extremely lucky. My parents always said, "Okay, well sure, you can have that if you want it, you just need to earn the money to buy it."

I remember when I was about six years old, I had a hand-me-down, beat-up old baseball mitt. And not a nice one. You can get a nice old leather mitt that arguably would be better because it's already worked in. But this was a cheap plastic mitt. I remember seeing other kids who had nicer, leather ones. I wondered, *How do I get one of those?* So like most kids at that age, I went to my mom—and I know a lot of moms would have been frustrated if they had a child who kept coming to them the way kids do. I understand why so many parents say things like, "Why can't you just be grateful for what you have?" or "Don't you know how hard we work to make sure you have what you need?"

But that was never my mom. I could go to her all excited and say, "Oh man, Justin has this new mitt and it was leather and it was bigger, and he could catch the ball better." And she'd get into it with me, matching my excitement. "Wow, that sounds amazing! That's so awesome."

And then I asked, "Well, can I get one of those?"

"Yeah, of course you can," she said.

"Okay . . . so, how do I get it?"

"You just save up your money and I'll take you to the store so you can buy it."

She never got negative. Instead, she made it almost like a game, a challenge. She built the dream right along with me.

Sometimes during conversations like these, especially as I made it out of toddlerhood, my parents were able to respond to my requests with actual opportunities to earn money. Having a job was something my parents wanted for us early on, to learn the value of work and earning money. Of course, at first, I wasn't necessarily thinking about getting a job. But my parents would come to my brother and me and say, "Hey, we can get a summer job for you guys so you can earn some money, if you want to." And we always wanted to. The feeling of earning our own money and spending it as we pleased was addictive.

As I got older I started to proactively look for ways to earn more, like cutting grass, selling baby chicks, or pulling a red wagon with items for sale around the neighborhood. I was still too young for a real job (though I did get my first one, a paper route, at age eight) but I was very motivated. When we lived in Vegas, we had a garden, and I would pick radishes, wash them, bundle them up, and go around door to door to sell them to people for twenty-five cents. One time, when we were at a family reunion, I noticed that someone was selling painted rocks. I couldn't believe it! I thought, *You've got to be kidding me, that's brilliant!*

So the first thing I did when I got home was go outside and gather a bunch of rocks and start painting them. I stacked them in my little red wagon and off I went. I remember I sold one of those rocks for a dollar, which seemed like a lot then. Who knows what anyone even did with those things? They probably just had a hard time saying no to a six-year-old kid!

Looking back, I understand how important it was that my parents encouraged me to have a job so that I could have money. Having my own money coming in on a fairly regular basis helped my brain to connect the dots: "I want this thing," "This thing that I want costs this much money," and finally, "Okay, so I have money, do I have enough and how much do I really want this thing?"

Of course, as a young child, I was still blissfully ignorant. As I said earlier, my parents helped me to see earning money as a fun challenge. It wasn't like, "You mean I'm going to have to work for it?" Instead, it was more like, "Oh that's all I have to do? Great."

And I was able to do it, every time. Sometimes it took longer, but I always believed I could, and I did. Aside from candy, the first thing I ever bought for myself was a baseball mitt.

The moral of all this is that if a child has the desire, and if the degree of desire is so high that he is willing to sacrifice, work hard, and be creative in order to acquire what he wants, then he will eventually get it. And it's exactly the same for you. I'm here to tell you, "Yes, you can have it. You just need to earn the money and go buy it."

You can, and you will, and this book will show you how.

Getting Permission

The day a billionaire sat in my car's passenger seat was a wakeup call for me. I was driving John Paul DeJoria—cofounder of the John Paul Mitchell hair care empire and owner of the Patrón Spirits Company, among other ventures—to the airport to board his private jet after he had toured our Paul Mitchell school in St. George, Utah. It was 2005, and John Paul had flown in to satisfy his promise to all Paul Mitchell franchisees to speak at each school's grand opening. This time, he addressed the crowd at the school I'd helped found after a chance lunch meeting with some friends of a friend turned into a business partnership. I watched along with hundreds of students and staff as John Paul recounted the amazing story of how he and his cofounder, Paul Mitchell, started their company with a loan of just seven hundred dollars, a car, and a trunkful of hair products.

Everyone was enamored of him, like he was a movie star. It isn't every day that people in a small town like St. George get to "rub elbows" with a billionaire, after all. I could see the awe people had just standing in the same room with him that day. I could feel it myself.

A few hours later, there I was, a kid from small-town USA, raised in a middle- to lower-income family, someone who had to fight and earn everything he had, sharing a private audience with one of the most powerful and wealthiest men in the world. I could still feel that awe, that buzz, from earlier. You often hear people who have met celebrities say stuff like, "He was just a normal guy." And it's true! John Paul was just like anybody else in so many ways, just a normal guy. Probably because he had such unimpressive beginnings. He grew up in an impoverished Los Angeles neighborhood; he and his brother had to live in a foster home when his mother found herself incapable of providing for them. He spent time in street gangs, cleaned himself up to join the navy, entered a training program with Redken, and ultimately founded his own business. He went on to grow incredible wealth for himself and his family.

After I dropped him off, my mind was swimming with thoughts. I thought about the many adversities John Paul had to overcome in building his success. With this success he inspired and influenced thousands of people and created meaning and value for millions of others. This man was truly a business icon who had done philanthropic work throughout the world, and it had moved me deeply to see how his very presence excited and inspired people.

I compared John Paul's humble beginnings with my own, and considered how far I'd come in building my own business "empire." I began with selling cell phones at age twenty-two, and though I quickly rose to become the company's top salesman, I struggled a bit with my self-confidence. I overcompensated for my young age by always coming to work in a suit and tie, and I even wore fake eyeglasses to try to look older and more sophisticated. What finally happened for me was that after about five years of outselling my peers and older coworkers, after holding the number one sales record in three different companies, winning awards and breaking records left and right, I finally felt like I had enough credibility to stop apologizing for my age.

My strong suit has always been in sales, creating revenue, and developing personnel and people. At age twenty-nine, when we brought the Paul Mitchell school to my hometown of St. George, I already had a couple of other businesses running profitably—mostly in the realm of financial services, helping entrepreneurs structure, establish, and grow their own businesses. And yet I hadn't accomplished the one thing I'd always dreamed of doing: I hadn't yet written a book.

But something about having this "normal guy" billionaire sitting in my car that day really clicked with me. It felt similar to when I decided I didn't need to act older than my age to earn respect. In a way, there wasn't much difference between John Paul and me. I hadn't yet achieved his level of success, but I believed that if he had done it, I could if I wanted to.

I understood at that moment that what I had learned and turned into several great successes (in business and in my personal life) *already had significant value*. I realized that I had an obligation to share with others what I knew and what I use every day. It was time for me to put pen to paper and share my own "secrets." John Paul had unknowingly given me the permission I needed to believe that I had something worthwhile to say to others. I started writing the outline of what would eventually become this book that very night.

People typically choose a profession because of someone in their life who had an impact on them. For me, that person was Zig Ziglar. He made me want to affect and influence the lives of other people in the same way that he did for me. And Zig always said that everyone should write at least one book in their lifetime. I always knew I would take his advice (I did about pretty much everything else!), but as I said, I felt I lacked the credibility somehow. Recognizing the similarities between John Paul and me, and fully embracing the power of knowing that I was partners with one of the world's great entrepreneurial minds, assured me that I was finally ready.

One of the most fulfilling and exciting things is to see someone you have influenced succeed and grow. That's the real reason why I've written this book. I am not naïve, and I fully expect some people to criticize my work. I am reminded of the people who thought Walt Disney was crazy, and I wonder who he thought about in his insecure moments of doubt. And you will experience those moments too, just like Walt Disney, just like John Paul DeJoria, just like me. *But I am giving you permission, right now, to believe in yourself, to achieve everything you've ever wanted to do, be, or have.*

This book, if read with an open mind, will change the way you look at life. To the many people who will read and apply this book and forever change their future and their posterity's future: this book is written for you.

What You Focus on, You Feed

The Cherokee parable of the two wolves offers powerful insight into the kind of personal turmoil I've been describing—that feeling of "not good enough," of needing someone else to tell you "Yes, you can" before you believe it yourself. It goes like this:

> One day an old Cherokee chief taught his grandson about life.
>
> "There is a terrible fight going on inside me. It's a terrible fight and it's between two wolves."
>
> The boy looked up at his grandfather expectantly. Grandfather went on. "One is evil; he is anger, regret, greed. He is arrogance, self-pity, guilt, resentment, inferiority, lies, false pride, superiority, self-doubt, and ego. The other is good; he is joy, peace, love, hope, serenity, humility, kindness, benevolence, empathy, generosity, truth, compassion, and faith." Grandfather took a breath, then said, "The same

fight is going on inside you and inside every other person, too."

The grandson thought about it for a moment, then asked, "Which wolf will win?"

Grandfather answered simply, "The one you feed."

What part of your life do you feed? What part of your life do you give the most attention? Do you look back and have a weekly pity party, or do you move forward embracing your challenges, anticipating the best? What happens in your life depends on what you focus on, what you feed.

Some people feel like they are "stuck" with their lot in life. That it cannot change. That the cards they were dealt are it. Some have been told, "You can't do it. You'll never succeed," so many times that unfortunately they believe it. Some have seen others try and fail and are not willing to risk the assumed embarrassment of failing, so they don't even try. Most people just go through the motions of what they believe (or don't believe) is possible or available to them.

Definition of *Belief* (*Collins English Dictionary*)

1. a principle, proposition, idea, etc., accepted as true

2. opinion; conviction

3. religious faith

4. trust or confidence, as in a person or a person's abilities, probity, etc.

You are where you are because that is what you believe is possible for you. You're asking now:

Do you mean that I believe I should be broke?

Do you mean that I believe I deserve to be unhappy?

Do you mean that I believe I cannot be healthy?

Do you mean that I believe I am destined to be overweight?

The answer is YES. That is exactly what I am saying!

Best-selling author and productivity expert Steven Covey says that the more awareness you have, the more aware you are of what you don't know. Take someone from small-town USA, and they probably think they know a whole lot—but that's only because these people don't know what they don't know. Their awareness is limited. But take someone who has two PhDs and a vast array of knowledge—she is acutely aware of everything she doesn't know! In this way, the most intelligent person on the planet is also the dumbest, because that person is completely aware of everything she doesn't know.

This book has steps that are repeatable for every goal, big or small, that you will have in life. I'm not just going to fire you up. You'll know exactly what to do. But this book is not just about achieving a goal and getting stuff. It's about what happens when you expand your awareness and change your beliefs—it's about the personal transformation that occurs along this journey. It's about what you feed, and what you don't.

What you don't understand today but what is absolutely true is that losing fifty pounds (or whatever your goal is) is not nearly as impactful or powerful as the person you have to become to lose that fifty pounds. That's really what happens with any goal. Making a million dollars is nothing compared to the person you have to become to earn that million dollars. That's what is life-changing. You have to have this awareness of everything you're doing, a purpose, an intention . . . it can't just be "I'm going to lose this weight." I think you already know that simply stating an intention isn't enough. You have to plan out your meals, think about what you're putting in your mouth, get up early to exercise, and so on. The discipline, the habits you create, the things you read, the people you talk to . . . all of it changes you even as it brings you close to your goal. When your awareness changes, that changes your beliefs; when your beliefs change, that changes you.

Paths don't just come cleared for everyone. You make your own path by removing what stands in your way. Stumbling blocks are a part of life, and when they appear you have several choices. You can stop and go back the way you came. You can move the obstacle, or you can build a bridge and simply "get over it." It's always a choice—it's always *your* choice. You are in charge of your destiny. And it all begins with the awareness that what you focus on, you feed. So let this be the very first moment of opening up your own awareness to the choices you make and the things you choose to focus on. Here's to a future in which you shape your life for the better by choosing to believe it is possible.

It's time to take control of your life.

HOW TO USE THIS BOOK

ARE YOU LOOKING to take control of your life? Of your future? Of your finances? Are you looking to grow your business? To start a business? Anyone looking to better their life financially, emotionally, physically, spiritually, mentally, and to have inner peace . . . This book is for YOU. If you are just starting out in your career, are in the middle or toward the end, this book is for you. If you struggle with believing in yourself and limit yourself to what others have told you is "acceptable" for you . . . This book is for you.

You can accomplish anything that you want to accomplish. You can do anything you want to do. You can be anything you want to be. That's what I want you to take away from reading this book. Not just to know or even believe it like a kind of "blind faith," but be able to connect the dots, A to B, B to C, C to D, on how to do it from a practical standpoint. Even though I talk a lot about "belief," this is not some "wishful thinking" or "I hope that this might be" guide—it contains actual advice and knowledge that's going to walk you through the steps of how to do anything you want to do. I'm going to show you how to cultivate belief in yourself, belief that anything is possible, and how to use it to propel you toward your goals.

I recommend that as you read this book you follow the action steps as prompted. As you read it, have a highlighter or pen handy so you can highlight or note the things you really like so that you can go back to them for inspiration later. At the end of each chapter you will find exercises designed to help make the concepts I'm teaching concrete for you and to give you a taste of their power right away. So as you are prompted to go through the activities, do them right then and follow through. If you do, you will see a result right away. It's immediate; it does not take time. I am not saying, "Hey, if you do this, then ninety days or a year from now you'll see a result." No. Again, it's immediate. Once you take that action, you'll start seeing the difference. And because of this, your outlook on life will be more hopeful than it has been in years.

I encourage you to ride that wave of positivity, but be wary of telling everyone you've ever known how awesome your life has become. I would say that if you choose to quit smoking or quit drinking or lose weight, these are things you should definitely share with people who will hold you accountable. But this book deals with other goals too— let's call these "dream goals." I'd be careful about whom you share these with because there are a lot of dream killers out there, naysayers who don't want you to move up or improve or win because that makes them look worse. You'll always be able to find someone who tells you why you can't do something. Be very protective of your dreams and don't share them with people who might try to kill them. Just work on those on your own.

You will also notice that in addition to the short exercises in each chapter, there is a workbook at the back of this book. The workbook will walk you through a full process—the same one that I use in my life and that I have shared with many others—to take you from identifying which goals you want to pursue to outlining a plan to taking action to, ultimately, achieving those goals. It begins with an important section on how to evaluate where you're at personally in multiple areas of your life: what I call the 7 Pillars. To know where you want to go, you have to know where you're at now.

But for now, just read the book. Absorb it. Try the exercises. And when you've completed all of that, use the workbook to create a road map toward whatever it is you want most in life, right now.

Now let's get started!

Chapter One

BE DUMB ENOUGH TO BELIEVE IT

Believe it can be done. When you believe something can be done, really believe, your mind will find the ways to do it. Believing a solution paves the way to solution.

— David Joseph Schwartz —

I DIDN'T MAKE the high school basketball team as a freshman. The coach, who was also my physical education teacher, generously told me I could fill the last spot on the team if I really wanted in, but that I would get very little playing time. I'm sure the fact that I was five feet, seven inches tall and weighed 108 pounds soaking wet had something to do with it. He encouraged me to instead try out for the wrestling team. He'd taught my class some wrestling throws in PE and, watching me, thought I had potential. I had two older cousins who wrestled, so I figured wrestling sounded good. And, I was "dumb" enough to believe that I had *potential!*

My wrestling coach was known as a drill sergeant. Seriously, though, one of the kids who wrestled for him went into the Marines and said, "Boot camp was easy compared to Coach's workouts!"

He would get into our heads. "Your opponents may have wrestled longer than you. They may be stronger than you. They may be smarter than you. *But they have not worked as hard as you have worked!* When your opponent is sucking for air and wishing he were dead, that is when the hard work pays off! That is when we win!"

Well, again, I was "dumb" enough to believe my wrestling coach. I certainly hadn't wrestled as long as the other kids. I definitely wasn't as strong as they were. So I worked hard. Real hard. Extremely hard.

Other people on the wrestling team said things like, "You're never going to make varsity. You're not good enough." "You just barely started wrestling and we've been wrestling since we were five years old." "Well, now you're doing great, but don't expect too much. You'll never place at State." If I'd listened to them, I never would have been any good, I never would have made varsity, and I never would have placed at State. But I didn't listen to them, because I believed my PE teacher when he told me I had potential, and I believed my coach when he said that if I just worked hard enough, I would be great. And eventually I did get good, I did make varsity, and I did place at State. So be "dumb" enough to believe.

Cultivating Hope

People get broken. It sounds strange when you put it that way, but it's true. Life beats up on you in many ways. Loss of family, loss of independence, loss of love, loss of possessions, loss of confidence: these things happen every day. How do you get beyond what you've lost or never had, to move toward believing?

Some journeys can be public, some private, but in every journey toward belief, the power of hope is what propels you forward.

Before you can even have a desire to believe—to be more, to do more, to want more—you have to have hope.

You may not feel very hopeful right now. That's okay. The fact that you got out of bed this morning proves hope lives in you. The fact that you are reading these words proves hope lives in you. Hope lives in all people, regardless of culture or country of origin. There are stories of hope to be found in the world, in your nation, in your community, down the street, even in your own family, against seemingly impossible odds. Hope is everywhere and is eternal.

Hope is powerful.
Hope in the present creates power in the future.
That is the promise of hope.

Hope will lead you to belief. Belief will increase your confidence. Belief will increase your self-worth. Belief will build your self-esteem. In the New Testament, Mark 9:23 says, "If thou canst believe, all things are possible to those who believeth."

If hope is the first step to believing, then when you hope you are moving forward. You are already starting to change.

Cream of the Crop

Rachel Pratt lived on an Indian reservation in southern Utah with her mother and six siblings. Rachel was seven years old the first time she and her six siblings were put in foster care. Their parents were divorcing and because of a looming custody battle, the kids were put into foster care for four months. They were then returned to their mother, who remarried after a short time.

Their stepfather abused them, particularly one of the boys. He burned his stepson's index finger to the bone, and eventually it became gangrenous. Rachel, who was almost ten, tried to care for her brother's finger, but in the end it was amputated to the first knuckle. Rachel learned to hide under her bed when strange men came into her house so she wouldn't be sexually molested. She learned to stay away from her abusive stepfather and did her best to help her siblings. She tried to stay away from the pornography that was everywhere. Life was pretty bleak.

One day, Rachel met a married couple who served as missionaries on the reservation. During her interaction with them, the woman gave her a hug and said, "You are the cream of the crop." She asked what that meant, and the woman's reply was, "You are special. You are the very best." Rachel had no idea why the woman said that to her, but she had said it with such love that Rachel knew it had to be true—this woman clearly believed it, and so Rachel believed it.

In Rachel's world, compliments came rarely, if ever. She was so busy trying to keep her siblings and herself safe, she never had the time to think of anything but what was right in front of her. But Rachel believed those words, and for the first time she saw a way out of the life on the reservation. If she was "the cream of the crop," then there must be a better future for her. This knowledge ignited hope that things would improve.

Six months after Rachel learned she was "the cream of the crop," Rachel's mother was killed in an accident. Again Rachel and her siblings were sent to foster care, as no one in her family wanted to take all seven children.

All of the children were placed in a home where there were already seven children. There was no bed for Rachel, so she slept on a door. No mattress, just a wooden door placed on the floor. But the hope Rachel had felt would not be extinguished. She chose to focus on the fact that she wasn't sleeping on the floor, because she had the door, and the door kept the roaches from getting to her. And she never forgot that she was "the cream of the crop."

Rachel's life came to be constantly in flux. When it was finally decided that fourteen children in one home didn't work, she and some of her siblings were put into other foster homes. After a time, she was sent back to the reservation, and shortly after that she returned to foster care. She never knew how long she would live with a family. She had come "home" more than once to discover she was being moved to another place.

Her constant turmoil ended when at sixteen she was placed with her biological father. Finally she had a permanent home! She was no longer worried that one day a social worker would tell her she had to move again. Her clothes were put into her own drawers and closet. She had a place where she belonged. A home with a father who wanted her to be there. She had believed that things would get better, and they had.

During all these years, she had held on to the belief that she was "the cream of the crop." Now that she had some semblance of a normal life, she felt the freedom to live up to the kind missionary's belief in her. She decided to get the best grades in high school, and she graduated with a perfect 4.0. Those words, "You are the cream of the crop," had stayed with her since she was a child. During her life, she'd seldom been given any positive reinforcement from anyone. She treasured those words from someone she hardly knew. She was "the cream of the crop"; she knew that there was something more for her; she applied to a local college because the application fee was only thirty dollars, and she was awarded an academic scholarship. Her hope burned brightly.

Rachel graduated with a dual major and now works with at-risk families. Her belief that she was "the cream of the crop" led her out of the reservation and toward an education. She could now take care of herself and those she loved. She could be more than she had been on the reservation, and now she could help others as that missionary had helped her long ago. The hope that led her to belief remains to this day. She never saw herself as a victim. From an early age she had hope, and with every step she took she was closer to a brighter future.

Today Rachel shares her hope with her families. As she says, she works with "the cream of the crop."

The power of hope is unending. Even in the darkest of times, hope can light the way. Even the faintest glimmer of hope can start a wildfire of change in your life.

To get to the point of belief, you have to hope that there is something better for you. Without that hope, you wouldn't be able to get out of bed in the morning. Stop and take time to think about the reason you got out of bed this morning. Was it for your children, for your job, for exercise? Why did you choose to read this book? Was it because you wanted to learn to believe? Was it because you were curious? Whatever the reason, these acts are manifestations of hope. They are proof that hope exists within you.

EXERCISE: What Gives You Hope?

Studies have shown that the following things give hope to people from around the world.

- A warm friendly smile
- Knowing that tomorrow is another day
- A baby's innocent face
- The laughter of children in the background
- A slow deep breath
- The sunrise on a quiet morning
- A dog wagging its tail
- The soft purr of a cat

- The sounds of ocean waves and the feel of sand between your toes
- Unconditional love
- Warm sunshine on a crisp autumn day
- A small act of kindness from a stranger
- A rainbow arching across the sky
- A heartfelt touch
- A full moon cresting over the mountain
- Listening to beautiful music
- The sound of crickets in the evening breeze
- The smell after it rains

Why do *you* have hope? Think about it: you have hope or you wouldn't be reading this book. What is it that gives you hope? Spend a little time thinking about it, and make a list. Keep going until you feel satisfied and uplifted.

Healing Is Proof

When you have the hope that tomorrow will be a brighter day, it gives you the courage, the willpower, to take action. The process that takes us from hope to belief is inextricably tied up with healing. After all, what better proof is there that things can get better than the fact of healing? Whether it's emotional, mental, or physical, to heal is to improve over time. In many cases healing happens without your even trying. In other cases, it may require a little attention. Either way, the point is that all things can heal. *You* can heal. Your relationships can heal. Healing is proof that there is something to hope for, that all things are possible. When you witness or simply accept the existence of healing, it cultivates hope. When you have hope, you heal those parts of you that are hurt or broken. And so on.

In order to start healing, you have to take care of the underlying problem. For example, if you severely cut your arm and it gushes blood, you need a qualified person to get the blood to stop. You can't stop it on your own (at least, not very well) because you don't have the knowledge. You need the help of a professional.

It's the same with the wounds of life. When you have a problem that is so severe, so traumatizing, that you can't handle it yourself, get professional help. You need to have an expert help you so you can see that you have hope. Someone who can listen to your problem, say you're not the only one, show you some examples, and in the end tell you, "Suck it up and get on with your life."

There are many ways to heal. An expert can be a valuable aid in healing. For some it might be a life coach, for others a therapist. For some it may be a financial advisor or a fitness expert. Working with an expert can help you define what you want, give you encouragement so you can accomplish what you want, and prop you up when you falter. An expert can guide you on the steps toward healing and then on toward your goal.

Once you take the first step forward, the healing process can and will begin. No matter how deep the original wound, it will heal with the proper treatment. It may take more time than you want, but it will heal.

No matter how the healing process works or feels, in the end when the metaphorical scab falls off there is new healthy skin. And new skin is yet another physical manifestation of hope.

Borrow Someone Else's Belief

By studying other people whom you admire, whom you adore, or who have a life you wish to emulate, you will see that there are things about you that are like them. Understanding that you have even one thing in common with someone you want to be like will give you hope. It can be something like the fact that he is a parent, he lives alone, or he is left-handed. It doesn't matter. Identifying some small intersection of your lives will give you hope.

I remember as a child listening to some of my parents' motivational recordings about network marketing. I was just six or seven, so I didn't complain about what my parents would put on. They were all good and inspiring, but one speaker stood out to me: Zig Ziglar. His positive attitude and upbeat energy were inspiring and fun to listen to, and Zig's voice stuck with me throughout my childhood.

Before a wrestling match, each athlete has his "ritual" and method for preparing to go into battle. Most of the kids would listen to hard rock or heavy metal before their match. While they were listening to their music, I was listening to Zig Ziglar. He would say, "You can do it! You just have to believe! You can get everything you want out of life if you just help enough other people get out of life what they want." He repeated that message over and over again. Maybe I was easily influenced. Maybe I was searching for something bigger than what my current circumstances allowed me. But I believed him.

Zig Ziglar became one of my best friends, confidants, and mentors, and he didn't even know it. I hadn't met him at that time, but his was the voice I would hear saying, "You can do it! You can do it! I believe in you! Focus, write it down, work toward it, and you can do it!" I leaned on his voice until I could hear my own. Just as Rachel borrowed the belief of the missionary, I borrowed Zig Ziglar's belief until I had belief in myself.

Some people will be "dumb" enough to believe they can do anything and will become the next Neil Armstrong or the president of the United States thirty years from now. Others have lacked belief in themselves for so long, they need someone to believe for them. My gift to you is this: I believe in you. I believe in you, and you can borrow my belief until you believe in yourself.

Get Immediate Results

What period of time will you need to try this in order to see if it's going to work for you? It starts working *immediately*! You will notice a difference immediately when you hope for a brighter day. When you have hope:

- You can succeed
- You can achieve your goals
- You can pay your bills
- You can make more money

- You can have an amazing relationship
- You can meet the right person
- You can have better health
- You can find work
- You can grow your business
- You can enjoy life
- You can have peace
- You can lose weight
- You can have higher self-esteem
- You can have more confidence
- You can let go of the past
- You can travel the world
- You can have more free time
- You can finally have what you want . . .
- You Can Believe
- You Can Believe
- You DO Believe

What you believe is what you will achieve. You determine your beliefs and you determine your actions. It's time to believe in you. It's time to see that you can have what you want and be whom you want; you just have to work for it.

You, yes, you, the one reading this book: Be "dumb" enough to believe what I'm telling you. Just be open enough to say, "Okay, I'm going to try this on and I'm going to see if it works for me." Acknowledge your hope that it is possible this will work. That's all you need to do. That is step one.

Chapter Two

DREAMING BIG

All our dreams can come true, if we have the courage to pursue them.

— WALT DISNEY —

O NE NIGHT I was taking my thirteen-year-old daughter to play with her friends, and my three-year-old came along with us. As we got out of the car, I said to my three-year-old, "Let's race!" We started racing on the lawn and, being her dad, of course I was letting her win. I told her, "You're so fast! You're so speedy!"

When we got to the end she said, "I'm so fast that I'm faster than you!"

At three years old she believes that she is faster than me. She's faster than her dad.

If you ask a group of adults, "How many of you are good at singing?" few hands will go up, if any. "How many of you are good looking?" Again, few hands will go up.

In 2004, "The Real Truth about Beauty: A Global Report—Findings of the Global Study on Women, Beauty and Well-Being" was released to the public. The study showed that most women did not consider themselves beautiful. In fact, only 2 percent of the women surveyed saw themselves as being beautiful. "Natural" or "average" were the words most used by women to describe themselves. Ownership of the word *beautiful* did not exist in most women throughout the world.

Go to a kindergarten class and ask, "How many of you are fast runners?" Every hand goes shooting up.

"How many of you are great artists?" Every hand goes shooting up.

"How many of you are good looking?" Every hand goes shooting up.

You need to go back to feeling like you did in kindergarten, before life beat you up. You have to believe that these things are possible for you. You start out with a list of what you want your life to be, and then "life" happens. You experience failure and setbacks. People tell you what you're worth or that you're worthless. You begin to modify your goals and vision based on what you're told. You're slowly forced into a small bubble: "I will only be able to . . ." Your goals shrink to fit what you've been told you can do.

Part of believing that you can achieve anything you want to do, be, or have is being able to dream up those desires in the first place. You need to recover your ability to dream big.

Believe without Limitation

Walt Disney's life was one of ups and downs but always filled with big dreams. His first company, Laugh-O-grams, went bankrupt, but Walt Disney still dreamed. His first major benchmark came as he won an Academy Award with the first-ever color cartoon. He followed this success with classics such as *Snow White and the Seven Dwarfs*, *Pinocchio*, *Fantasia*, *Dumbo*, and *Bambi*. With all of these successes, Disney's dreams only continued to grow. Disneyland, a clean, family-oriented amusement park, opened next, followed by the first full-color programming on television. And still Walt Disney dreamed. Walt Disney World theme parks were built across the globe. And still he dreamed. And not only did he dream, his dreams kept growing even after his death. The Disney Company keeps dreaming, just as Walt Disney did.

Sure, there were times when people didn't believe he could do it, but Walt Disney believed. Even after his first company went bankrupt, he started again, and this time he won an Academy Award. I'm sure that there were people who told him he'd reached the top, but he kept going, because he dreamed, and he dreamed big. The only limits on you are the limits you place on yourself. And limits can douse dreams. You have to believe. You have to believe without limitation, without reserve.

Gold Medal on the Monkey Bars

Gabby Douglas was the first black American to win the all-around gold in the 2012 Olympics, and she did it by dreaming big. Her story began when she was three and taught herself a cartwheel. By the time she was four she'd taught herself a one-handed cartwheel and began gymnastics training. No one told her she couldn't or shouldn't do a one-handed cartwheel. She had watched her older sister and simply did what she saw her sister do. By age eight she had won the Level Four All-Around Gymnastics title at the Virginia State Championships. She didn't know she couldn't do it. She just did it.

For the next six years she continued her gymnastics training. When she was twelve she made her first national appearance at the U.S. Classic in Houston, Texas. This event is well known as the beginning of the road for many future Olympians. The following year she broke her wrist at the growth plate, and by the end of the year she had competed in only two events, the balance beam and the floor exercise. And yet she continued to train. At age fourteen, with her Olympic dreams growing, she moved away from home to train with Liang Chow, Olympic champion and coach of Shawn Johnson, a U.S. Olympian. Gabby trained daily, went to competitions, and in 2010 was part of the U.S. team that won the Pan-Am gold medal in gymnastics. According to a June 2012 *Los Angeles Times* article, her aim was to be the first African American woman to win an individual gold medal at the Olympics.

When speaking to ESPN in June 2012, Gabby said she visualized every routine before she did it. Before the 2012 Olympic team tryouts she said, "I visualized the floor set I wanted to do, and then I went out and hit the best floor routine of my life. It proved to me how powerful my mind can be." She visualized every routine before she performed it, saying, "You have to dream big and I do visualize myself standing on the top of the podium in London." Gabby's dreams never wavered. With time, her many goals—making a splash on the national level, training with an elite coach—became the stepping stones on her way to her ultimate goal: winning the gold medal.

An adult might watch Olympic swimmer Michael Phelps winning all those gold medals and be in awe. But I promise you, there is a kid somewhere in the world watching Michael Phelps and saying, "I will be the next Michael Phelps."

My question to you is, "When does an Olympic athlete believe he can win the gold medal?" Is it after he's begun to master the sport or when he's won a few events?

The answer is: Before he starts training. Otherwise, why would he go through the hell and the misery of training eight hours a day for four to eight years? He believes, even before training, that he can do it.

Visualization

Which world heavyweight championship boxer correctly predicted the outcome of seventeen out of nineteen fights? Is it a current fighter, one who has the expertise of a sports psychologist in his corner? No, it is Muhammad Ali, gold-medal-winning boxer in 1960. Calling visualization "future history," he used this skill not only to predict the outcome of fights but to also predict the round in which he would win.

Muhammad Ali used a combination of mental practices including visualization, affirmation, mental rehearsal, and self-confirmation. He combined all of these skills into one thought that perhaps is the most powerful affirmation ever: "I am the greatest!"

Before a fight, Ali mentally practiced every movement he would or could make before he ever stepped into the ring. Because he mentally performed every move possible, nothing ever came as a surprise. Everything he did in the ring, he had done before. This is the power of visualization, a critical component in the achievement of any goal.

Using this technique, along with hard work and training, Ali arguably became the world's greatest boxer just as he always said he was. Even before he truly believed he would achieve his dream, he said it out loud. He said it until he could believe it. He said it until it was reality. Ali did not limit his dreams in the slightest. One of his most famous quotes is, "The man who has no imagination has no wings." He gave himself freedom to achieve everything and anything he wanted. He had no boundaries that defined his success.

Numerous studies have been done on athletes who use visualization as part of their training. There is a reason why this works. When you visualize doing something perfectly and visualize the end result exactly as what you want it, your brain believes it. During your visualization, the neurons fire in your brain as they do when you are physically performing the action, thus creating neural patterns in your brain. Let me repeat that so it's clear: *Visualization trains your brain.*

Mary Lou Retton, the 1984 Olympic champion gymnast, also used visualization to achieve her dream of winning a gold medal. According to a *Time* magazine article, the night before the 1984 women's gymnastics finals, sixteen-year-old Retton lay in bed visualizing the perfect vault. The fact that she had just had knee surgery had no impact on her visualization of success. She had visualized herself performing each of her routines perfectly hundreds of times for years. Now, despite her recent surgery, she visualized her next day's performance in detail: who would be watching, what the arena looked like, how loud the crowd would be before and after her perfect vault. She saw herself preparing, felt the chalk on her hands, felt her feet running, felt her hands on the horse, and felt the air hitting her face as she vaulted upward. She knew the sound her feet would make as she stuck the landing. She heard the screams of the fans and the sound of her coach's voice. She smiled as she visualized herself on the Olympic podium receiving the gold medal, felt the weight of the medal around her neck, and heard herself singing the national anthem.

In the end, she won the gold medal, having not one but two consecutive perfect scores of ten on the vault.

Visualization can and will prepare you for success in your life, in your goals, and in achieving your dreams. In 1977, Natan Sharansky, a computer specialist accused of spying for the United States, was sentenced to imprisonment in the USSR for nine years. During that time he played mental chess with himself. Because of his circumstances, he had to be able to visualize what he wanted. He decided, "I might as well use the opportunity to become the world champion." For years he visualized chess matches—every move, every countermove—but played no physical chess. In 1996, ten years after being released, Sharansky beat the world champion chess player Garry Kasparov in an exhibition in Israel, once again proving that the mind can be as powerful as it can be limiting. It's all up to you.

EXERCISE: Visualization on Reaching Higher

Now I want you to stand up, keeping your legs straight, and I want you to give it your very best shot and reach up as high as you possibly can. Remember that spot. Now this time I want you to visualize yourself reaching even farther; close your eyes and imagine yourself reaching farther, imagining how it feels, what it looks like, maybe even the sound your body makes. Open your eyes, and this time I want you to stretch even farther than you did the first time—stretch—reach as high as you possibly can! Go for it!

Did you reach farther the second time than the first time? Why? Go back and read the previous paragraph again. I asked you the first time to reach as far as you possibly could; how is it that thirty seconds later you were able to reach even higher?

Consider how you will apply this technique to your bigger goals in life. For now, practice visualizing the details of whatever you want to achieve. Use all of your five senses to make the visualization as real as possible. Do this every morning and every night. It will happen for you, and you will know it when it happens, because you've "seen" it before.

How Do YOU Dream?

Maybe you've spent your life listening to people who told you, "Oh that's ridiculous, that's just a pipe dream," as though your dreams weren't even worth having. Well, let's start undoing that negative programming. When talking about today's successful entrepreneurs, *Forbes* magazine has noted that every successful person dreamed, and continues to dream, big. According to *Forbes*, there are four components to dreaming big: Dream Bold, Dream Specific, Dream Concise, and Dream Consistent.

Dream Bold. If you were to look at the career of Steve Jobs, you would see that his dreams were beyond what anyone thought was possible. He dreamed that Apple would become the greatest consumer electronics company in the world. With the introduction of the iPod and iTunes, he changed the way consumers purchased music. With the iPhone, he changed the way consumers used their phones, while changing the way phone companies did business. In the past the phone companies told the phone manufacturers what they wanted, but with the onset of the iPhone it was Apple telling phone manufacturers what the phone required. Now that's a pretty Bold Dream.

Dream Specific. Have a dream and attach a deadline to it. Deadlines create massive action. In 1983 Steve Jobs said he would like to "put an incredibly great computer in a book that you can carry around with you and that you can learn how to use in 20 minutes." Can you say *iPad*, anyone?

Dream Concise. *Concise* means "short and to the point"; think of something that would fit in a Twitter post. Steve Jobs saw the opportunity in apps and wanted to create a system that would prove robust enough to help the iPhone or iPad user do practically anything he or she wanted to do. And so the famous Apple slogan "There's an app for that" was born. Steve Jobs wanted "There's an app for that" to be every Apple user's reality. To make your dream your reality, you have to know exactly what it is. You have to be able to take the steps necessary to fulfill your dreams, and in order to do that you have to know exactly where you're going. Saying "I want to be happy" isn't a concise dream. "I want to be married with two kids and own my home" is a concise dream. With the latter, you can start taking steps to achieve these specific and tangible goals. By doing that, you create stepping stones to your ultimate goal, which is to be happy.

Dream Consistent. Steve Jobs was never one to rest on his laurels; before he died, he dreamed of creating an iCar. He never stopped dreaming, even when facing his impending death from cancer. When he achieved one dream, he reached for a new one that would build on his success. When you dream consistently, your dreams almost take on a life of their own. In the case of Steve Jobs, he left his dreams for others as a foundation for their own dreams. The more you achieve, the more you will dream, and so on. With each success comes more belief in your ability to achieve those dreams, because success is the bedrock for higher ground.

Think of some people who are successful. Were they always successful, or were there ups and downs? The one thing I know you will find in everyone who is successful is that they dreamed bigger than anyone thought possible. And one dream led to another, so they were always growing, always dreaming, and always finding a way to make dreams come true.

EXERCISE: Dream Bigger

What's your dream home? Yes, I want you to think of the perfect place for you. It can be anything you want, anything at all. If you've always wanted to live in a tree house with all the comforts of new technology, write it down. If you want to live on a lake with magnificent 360-degree views, write it down. If you want to live in an apartment in New York City, write it down.

1. **Dream Bold.** Don't give yourself any limits. Don't try to limit your dream home to what you think you can afford, or even what you think you deserve, or what you're capable of earning or maintaining. Think of it as though you just won the lottery. If money were no object, if you could have absolutely anything you want, what would your house look like?

2. **Dream Specific.** Now take it a step further. How many square feet is the home exactly? You said that you wanted a big closet for your clothes. Well, how big? Is the closet as big as your living room is now? What does that look like? What type of flooring do you have in the house? Where would your kitchen be located, and what appliances are in that kitchen? Would the appliances be stainless steel? What about the cupboards? What would they look like? What type of silverware would you use? To aid you with this step, I want you to create a "dream board." Go and get some magazines. Go through them and cut out everything that

you want in your dream home. As you do this, imagine each exact thing being in your dream home. If it's not what you want, throw the picture out. If it is what you want, glue it to a dream board. This board will represent your dream house. You now know where you want your house, how large it will be, what the interior will look like, and even what will be in your home.

3. **Dream Concise.** Now that you've gotten specific about what you want in your dream home, it's time to create a concise statement that captures your goal. It needn't include all of those details, but it should be specific. So for example, "My dream home is huge and beautiful and filled with expensive furniture" is too vague to be effective, though it is concise. Instead, you'd want something like "My dream home is a 4,500-square-foot Victorian overlooking a valley in central New York, with updated amenities and a kitchen the size of my current bedroom." Focus on the details that are the most important to you.

4. **Dream Consistent.** You don't want to give your subconscious mind mixed messages, so once you're clear on your dream, stick to it. You don't want to waffle between "Well, I think I'd be happy just living in a mobile home" and wanting to live in Cinderella's castle. It might be helpful to go and see homes like your dream home so that you can be absolutely certain it's what you want. When you are, revisit your dream in all the details (your dream board will help a lot here) daily.

Life Is More Than Peanut Butter

If, when you were growing up, your parents gave you only peanut butter sandwiches to eat, the only food you would know would be peanut butter sandwiches. Imagine that one day your aunt gave you a peanut butter and jelly sandwich—suddenly you have something *different*, something delicious. From that day on, you would want peanut butter and jelly sandwiches, because you now know there is more than peanut butter. You would not be satisfied until you had peanut butter and jelly sandwiches. You might even try peanut butter and pesto, and you might or might not like it. It doesn't matter, because you tried something new. You don't have to eat the peanut butter and pesto sandwich—if you don't like it, you can throw it away. But now you know you don't like peanut butter and pesto, and you can cross that off your list. There are plenty more things to try, plenty more things you will love, and plenty more that you don't want to repeat. But now you are on your way to finding out what makes you happy.

Find more to your life than just peanut butter, because it's out there for you. You have to see and want more than peanut butter. Your life is a virtual buffet for you to choose from.

I have three daughters, and our dinner talk is often about what their futures hold. One of my daughters wants to groom dogs. I told her, "That's great. You can learn all about it, all the ins and outs, and then own a grooming business!"

Another daughter wants to work at a pet hotel, and I told her, "Wonderful, then you can learn all about pet hotels and eventually start your own company!"

I already have my daughters thinking differently. Yes, there is a process they will have to go through, but I'm already brainwashing them into looking at owning a business rather than trading hours for dollars.

If my daughters never knew they could own businesses, they might grow up to happily groom and care for pets and that's all. But now they know they can own the businesses they want to work in, and so they are more likely to strive to become business owners. You have to see it to desire it. Once you desire it, and you believe you can have it, it becomes a very powerful belief. A belief takes you to creating a habit. Habits and beliefs joined together become very powerful. We'll talk more about how habits fit into the picture in Chapter Eight.

One last word about the importance of realizing that life is more than peanut butter: You must understand the difference between true desire and wishful thinking. True desire burns from within. It is something you cannot live without, something that you must have in order to feel whole. Wishful thinking, on the other hand, is something you think of in passing. If somebody goes to a piano recital, listens to the beautiful music, and says, "I wish I could play like that," does she really mean it? Or is it just a fleeting thought or wishful thinking in the moment? Because if she is willing to put in forty hours a week, learn the skills from a piano teacher, and practice until she achieves the 10,000 hours discussed in Chapter Seven, she *can* play like that.

When you really truly desire something, you study it. You want to know everything there is to know about it. As you gather more information, you find others who were once like you, who had your desire. When you see that someone else had your desire and then accomplished it, you will believe—because if it could happen for them, it can happen for you.

But again, you have to know that something exists in order to desire it. If all you've ever eaten is peanut butter, and you never knew about jam, all you would ever desire is peanut butter. Life is more than peanut butter. You have to open up your mind to more than what you see in front of you.

EXERCISE: Your Focus Becomes Your Reality

Whatever you focus on will become your reality. If your focus is on earning more money, you will see more opportunities to learn about increasing your earnings or see opportunities to make more money. If your focus is on losing weight, you will notice apps for losing weight and gym membership deals. You will be drawn to making healthy choices and shy away from fast food.

Have you ever bought a car thinking you were one of only a few to buy that make model and color? Then when you drive out of the dealership the first car you notice is one just like yours! Then you see another and another. Is it because suddenly everyone just bought the same car? Of course not. It's because you're now more aware of that car—you're focused on it, because you just bought one. Your sense of reality has expanded.

I have a little test for you. Right now, look around the room and find every item that is the color blue. How many blue items did you see? More than you thought you would? Count them all. Really think about it, so you get it right. Got them all? Good.

Now, how many yellow items did you see? What, you didn't know you were supposed to look for yellow?

See how it all has to do with what you are looking for. You missed the yellow because you were focused on the blue. Now if you look around the room again, you will be focused on yellow items; they will seem to jump out at you.

But now, how many red items did you see?

Be Careful, Your Heart Could Explode

Roger Bannister was the first person to run a mile in less than four minutes. Back in 1954, people generally believed that the human body was incapable of such a feat. A record of 4 minutes and 1.3 seconds had existed for nine years. The long-held belief that a running a four-minute mile was impossible kept many from attempting it, but Roger Bannister *believed* he could do it. He didn't accept the premise that it was impossible. As a medical student, he understood the human body. He made a plan and then proceeded to follow his strategy. He broke through the psychological barrier by using scientific training methods and by researching the mechanics of running. In the past, the great runners used hard repeat workouts, but Roger Bannister chose speed-building interval training and periodic rest breaks to allow his body time to heal. Both of these methods, race-specific training and enhancement of recovery, seemingly radical ideas at that time, are now the staples of most runners.

Once Roger Bannister ran a four-minute mile, other people started to do it too. He showed them that it was possible, and he showed them *how* it could be achieved. Now high school kids are running a mile in less than four minutes. Before Roger Bannister, people said, "Your heart will explode; it's physically impossible." Roger Bannister believed it in his own mind, conceived a plan, and made it happen.

Dreams Change Reality Every Day

Before Henry Ford could build a vehicle, he had to believe there was something like a carriage that wouldn't require horses. His dream of building a car that middle-class Americans could afford became a reality. He then made it possible to mass-produce an automobile at an affordable price and to have franchise dealerships throughout the country while paying workers a decent salary. He dreamed big, he dreamed specific, he dreamed consistent. I'm sure he could have told you very concisely what his dream was, too. But none of this came easily. He left the first company he formed and began a new company with a partner. He weathered the hard times, all the while keeping his belief intact. In the end, he achieved his initial dreams and sought even more success.

When I was a kid, the Commodore 64 computer came out. It was the biggest thing. Everyone wanted one. Now you see them in museums along with the rotary phone. Today, smart phones and tablets give people computers in their hands: fast, portable, stylish—and with more access to way more information more quickly than the Commodore 64. Twenty years ago, the general public would have never thought this scenario possible. But some tech geniuses believed, conceived a plan, and then worked at their plans until they were successful. And look how reality has changed.

The point is simple: people have to "see" or believe something will happen before it can happen. Don't ever be afraid to dream big. No matter how people laugh or criticize, now you know the truth—dreaming big is a critical part of every major success story. It will be part of yours, too.

Chapter Three

WHAT'S STOPPING YOU?

If you think you can do a thing or think you can't do a thing, you're right.

— HENRY FORD —

A YOUNG FOOTBALL PLAYER had a question most athletes have at one time or another in their lives. He went to his coach looking for advice.

"Coach," the young athlete said, "Am I going to be good enough to play in the professional league?"

His coach looked at the young man and asked, "Do you believe there will be a league in two years?"

"Of course I do," the young athlete said.

The coach then asked, "Do you believe there will be players for that league?"

"Yes. There will be players for the league."

The coach paused for a moment. "Somebody has to do it, why not you?"

The Psychology of Fear

Imagine you've pedaled your way to the crest of a hill and are beginning the descent. Traveling at thirty miles per hour, with only a plastic helmet to protect you, you lean close to find the most aerodynamic position and then the unimaginable happens. Your bike skids on the road, and you feel yourself falling, sliding across the asphalt. You skid, and when you look down you see innumerable injuries, luckily nothing too serious, but boy are you banged up. You look over at your bike and wonder what in the world ever propelled you toward riding at such high speeds. Then comes the thought, "How am I going to get back?" The bike isn't an option because you are too afraid to get back on. So here you sit and wonder what you should do next.

How do you get over the fear and back on the bike? Magnify this moment by ten and you have the reality of the professional bicycle racer.

Sports psychologist Julie Emmerman deals with this situation on a daily basis. "Most athletes tend to look at their thoughts and how they affect their behavior and mood," she says in *Mind Games: The Psychology of Fear*. "Over time, our brains adapt so that we remember painful things and we know in the future to stay away from them. So it makes sense from an adaptive point of view that when you crash you have an adverse reaction to that. It takes some reworking to train yourself to re-member that it's okay, that it is safe to do that thing again, and to have confidence in yourself."

Emmerman uses *mindfulness theory* while working with professional cyclists. Mindfulness is awareness with attention to present events and experience. "The mindfulness theory training I give involves teaching people to notice their reactions without judgment," she says. "If you can just deal with the feeling that you're feeling in the moment, and you don't have to have that secondary, 'Oh my gosh, there it is again,' or 'Crap, I'm freaking out again,' it's so much easier. If you can notice it, not judge it, not indulge in it, then it helps people because they realize it's just a feeling, they can stay above it. I often use the analogy of the CNN screen: your goal is in the main screen with Anderson Cooper, and the distractions are the ticker tape underneath. So as you're ap-proaching the scary descent it might be harder to stay in that main screen because your fear wants to jump down, but if you practice simply noticing that process and recognizing that it's happening, you can keep things in perspective."

In other words, fear is a natural part of life, but it doesn't have to control you. You can ignore that ticker at the bottom of the screen—fear can be overcome. In order to conquer fear you need to use all the tools in your toolbox—hard work, awareness, adaptation, innovation, and everything else you have at your disposal. But there can be times when you just have to move on and get over it.

"Sometimes you do just have to tell an athlete, 'Buck up!' It's not all such sophisticated psychology here," Emmerman says. "Sometimes you do need to say, 'You're really not taking responsibility for this and I know that you've come to me for help, but you need to—you can insert a number of phrases here—and unless you do, it's not going to work no matter what I do.'"

Just as with achieving any other goal, you have to have the desire to overcome your fear in order to succeed. That first step can be a doozy, because it's almost a leap of faith that you will conquer what holds you captive. Fear can and will become a part of you unless you choose to break away. You need to identify exactly what you are afraid of, so you can make a plan to overcome.

So how do you learn to not be afraid of something that hurt you in the past or is causing pain in the present? How do you train yourself to have confidence in yourself? Emmerman says, "You can give people skills to practice. It's very important to make the athlete feel his or her sense of empowerment. I have a lot to offer, but that person needs to take it and run with it. I'm not here to foster dependency. Here is a person who is self-sufficient, who is extremely powerful in his own right, something has happened like an injury, now let's supplement the toolbox so he can be on his way."

Did you notice the word *skills* in the preceding paragraph? There are skills to help you overcome your fear. They are skills you should have in your toolbox of life. You are powerful and can move on. You will learn the skills you need and you will move on. I'm giving you some of those skills right now!

As you heal both physically and mentally from the imagined bike ride—really any damaging situation you face in life—it's also time to free yourself from fear. It's so easy to magnify the moment to the point where fear is all you see. You forget that you've taken that ride a hundred times and not fallen. All you focus on is the last time, the time you fell. Remember, what you focus on becomes your reality. You have to get real with yourself and put your memories in order. Even in the case that you've fallen a hundred times, you need to focus on what causes the fear, piece by piece. Find out where it breaks down. Find the problem, and then fix it. Then you can shift your focus to getting back on that bike.

EXERCISE: Mind Games

It's night and your home is dark. You hear a tapping on your window. You have two choices: hide under the covers or turn on the light to see what it is. The logical choice is to turn on the light, and when you do, you find that a tree branch is hitting your window. You now know that in order to stop the tapping, tomorrow you need to trim the tree. You would have never known that if you had stayed under the covers in fear.

I'd like you to write down three things you are afraid of, ideally with regard to your current goals and dreams. Make them concrete and specific.

After you write those things, I want you to say each one out loud.

Then I want you to say, "Others have been afraid and have moved on. Why not me?" Go on, say it out loud right now. Better yet, look in the mirror while you say it.

Look at your fears in a logical manner. Look at them because you are now going to beat these limiting beliefs. When you bring your fear into the light, it will lose its grip on you. When you can clearly see what you are afraid of, you can take action steps to overcome your fear.

For example, suppose your fear is that you will not succeed at losing twenty pounds. Write it down.

Then say, "My fear is that I will not be able to lose twenty pounds."

Then I want you to go and read a success story of someone like you who has lost twenty pounds. What's the difference between him and you? Very little, if any.

Now say to yourself, "He succeeded and so will I."

Fear of Failure

It's never failure itself that stops people from succeeding; it's always *fear* of failure. The fear is what freezes them. The fear keeps them from taking the steps to action. When you fear failure, you also fear success. You have to know that failure is integral to success. It's how you deal with the inevitable failure that is the key. When you fail, you will try again, but this time you'll know more and achieve more.

So many people are afraid of failure. I say, "Be dumb enough to believe it." Michael Jordan once said, "You miss 100 percent of the shots you don't take." I get so frustrated with people who won't try. It's like someone told them early in life they were great at something. Now they're afraid they won't live up to the hype.

Get over yourself. The only way you get better at something is to try.

Listen, I often come up with ideas, lots of them. I know that most of the ideas will be horrible, but that doesn't stop me from throwing them out there and looking at them, considering them. I'm going to keep throwing them until a good one comes out: something that is going to make a difference. The ones that didn't work don't matter. They just get thrown in the junk pile and recycled. Keep putting it out there. One idea leads to another and another. Don't ever stop. Many species of sharks will die if they quit swimming. Your dreams will die if you don't keep working on them. Be a shark and keep swimming.

My thirteen-year-old daughter recently played in a basketball game. The team didn't practice much beforehand, and unsurprisingly they lost 16–4. When she came off the court she said, "Dad, let's face it. We stink."

I shook my head. "No," I told her. "It's not that you guys stink, it's that you didn't practice. What do you expect? You looked good out there. Your hair looked good and you had cute uniforms, but you didn't practice." The next week she went to basketball practice. After the next game, which I unfortunately had to miss, she said, "Dad you'd be so proud of me. We lost our game by ten points but I just kept shooting. My coach said you'll never score if you don't shoot, so I kept shooting, even though I didn't make one basket. " And I was very proud indeed!

That's the ticket, the whole thing in a nutshell. Keep swimming, keep shooting. No matter what it is in life, just keep trying.

Failure, or lack of success, is all part of success. Few people, if any, succeed with the first or even second try at something new. It's the ability to adapt, the ability to innovate that separates the successful person from the nonachiever. There is a saying: "I am a great believer in luck, and I find the harder I work, the more I have of it." Samuel Goldwyn, the great film producer from MGM, put it more succinctly: "The harder I work, the luckier I get."

EXERCISE: Comparing Stories

Many of the stories in this book are all about incredibly successful people who overcame failure. Not only did they overcome failure, they learned from failure. Failure for them was not the end game. They knew success would result from working hard and never giving up.

Choose one or two people who have achieved dreams and goals similar to what you want to achieve, or even just people you admire. Read their stories. As you do, make a list of all the obstacles, setbacks, and failures they struggled with on their way to success.

Now consider your own story thus far. Make a list of your own obstacles, setbacks, and failures. Add to the list the failures you're afraid of.

You can compare these lists side by side or just get a sense of the context of the other people's failures and fears versus your own. See how similar your story is to those of successful people? The only real difference is that they have already achieved their dreams, and you are still in the process of achieving yours. But it happened for them, and it will happen for you, too, if you believe it will.

We are a sum of our life experiences. If you never play, you may never get hurt, may never fail (whatever *failure* means to you), but you will never grow. Let's look more closely at just one of your goals. On the left side of a piece of paper, write down all the obstacles you can imagine. On the right side, write two or three things you can do to overcome each obstacle—and borrow some ideas from those other successful people's stories! If you can't see a way to overcome your obstacles, you need to start your research. There is nothing you want to do that someone else hasn't done. For every obstacle you face, you should have at least three ways to overcome that obstacle. Be creative, be inventive, and look beyond the obvious. Find your answers however you need to, knowing that there are ways to overcome every obstacle in your path.

For example, if one of your obstacles is a lack of money. overcome that by getting another job, making a tighter budget, and using your "eating out" money to fund your goal. If none of those options is available, start your research. Many successful people started with nothing. Yet they succeeded. Find out how they did it, then write it down on your list. Whatever they did was successful, and it will be successful for you. Write it down, and then DO IT!

Fear of Looking Dumb

Two mules were walking up a hill. The older mule was going slowly and occasionally slipping on the rocks. He'd shake, readjust the pack on his back, and continue on. The younger mule walked behind and kept slipping on the rocky slope. He shook a few times and kept walking and slipping. They came to a steep area and the older mule fell to his knees, found his footing, and got back up. The younger mule fell and slipped down the mountain twenty feet. As he lay there he called out, "What's the use? I just keep falling!" The older mule grunted and moved upward before answering, "Get up, kid. You've got a mountain to climb." The younger mule stayed down. The older mule stopped and looked back. "If you don't get up you'll get eaten by wolves. Your choice." The younger one answered, "It's hard and I keep falling." The older mule answered, "Like I said, your choice," and continued his climb. The young one called out, "I don't know how to climb like you." The older one continued on, "It doesn't matter how you get there, just get there."

Night began to fall and the younger mule was by himself as the older mule had climbed to the top. The wolves began to howl and the young mule was scared. Suddenly, he didn't care how he got up the hill, just as long as he got away from the wolves to safety. When he reached the top, the older mule stood to the side waiting. "Took ya long enough." The younger mule said, "I must have looked pretty stupid running up the way I did." The older mule answered, "Don't know. I was too busy getting up the hill."

How many of you are young mules too afraid to look dumb to folks who probably aren't even watching? You don't move until the wolf is at the door. Get over yourself. Nobody's watching. Everybody's too busy getting up the hill.

A True Athlete

Alana Nichols has always been an athlete, playing all kinds of sports including T-ball and soccer. When she was fourteen years old she started snowboarding. She loved to do tricks and aerials. After practicing for a summer, she decided to go up in the backcountry before the resorts opened. She and her friends built a practice jump. What she didn't know was that her landing area was above rocks. She overrotated on a flip and landed on her back atop a large rock. She couldn't feel her legs and feet and knew that something was seriously wrong.

After arriving at the hospital, she learned that she was paralyzed and that if she were ever to get the feeling back in the lower half of her body, it wouldn't happen for about two years. She was seventeen years old at the time of her accident.

She spent the next two years mourning her losses. One day she passed a game of coed wheelchair basketball. In her interview in January 2014 with *Women's Health* magazine, she said that because of her previous sports successes she felt "too proud to consider it." She had been a "true athlete" before.

But as she watched the wheelchair basketball, she saw that this sport required athleticism and began thinking about the idea of competing. Eventually she joined the team and transferred to the University of Arizona to join a collegiate women's wheelchair basketball team.

She continued with her wheelchair basketball and made the Women's Paralympic basketball team for the 2008 Olympics in Beijing. Before leaving for the Paralympics she went to Winter Park, Colorado, to visit the National Sports Center for the Disabled and said, "If I went to Beijing and won a gold medal I'd use the winning money to move to Colorado and pursue the Vancouver 2010 Paralympics in skiing." She did win the medal in Beijing with the basketball team and moved to

Colorado.

The ski coach told her to try for the 2014 Olympics, but Alana stuck to her plan and won two gold medals, a silver medal, and a bronze medal in the 2010 Vancouver Paralympics in skiing.

Once Alana decided to "get over" her fear of not being a "true athlete" she excelled. Today she continues to excel and inspire others.

A New Way to Look at Challenges

When you read the word *challenged*, it has a positive ring to it. You don't think of being challenged as being purely negative. You think of it as a test for success—something to be overcome, to be mastered. The word *failure*, on the other hand, can come with negativity. Failure has connotations with defeat. But what if you think about it this way? Failure is also something to be overcome and to be mastered. Failure is just facing another challenge. When you start out thinking about failure in terms of how you're going to overcome it, you're already starting to turn the situation around.

Not many people think of a hero or heroine in terms of failure. But stop and think about the fact that many heroes and heroines have themselves dealt with situations of defeat. Most of them have failed, not just once, but many times. We find their heroism in the fact that they got back up and the fact that they didn't allow failure to define them or their legacies. Their very heroism lies in the fact that they've faced failure and overcome it. The only failure I know is the one where you don't try. Then, and only then, have you indeed failed.

In the movie *Rocky Balboa* (*Rocky VI*), Rocky talks to his son, who is struggling with his father's choices. "Let me tell you something you already know. The world ain't all sunshine and rainbows. It's a very mean and nasty place, and I don't care how tough you are, it will beat you to your knees and keep you there permanently if you let it. You, me, or nobody is gonna hit as hard as life. But it ain't about how hard you get hit. It's about how hard you can get hit and keep moving forward; how much you can take and keep moving forward. That's how winning is done! Now, if you know what you're worth, then go out and get what you're worth. But you gotta be willing to take the hits, and not be pointing fingers saying you ain't where you wanna be because of him, or her, or anybody. Cowards do that and that ain't you. You're better than that!"

The point is, hits cannot be avoided. There are going to be things in life that try to knock us down. Our morale, our pride, and our self-worth are all prone to hits. The way to overcome them is not to block them out, or turn away from them. Picture Rocky in the ring—if he turns away from his opponent, he'll only be knocked down. If he doesn't get back up, he loses the fight. Obviously he's saying the same thing to his son as it pertains to real life. In order to get to where you want to go, you have to be willing to take the hits. You have to be willing to take the hits and get back up. You have to be willing to take the hits and not point fingers. You have to go on.

I like the way Rocky begins the quote: "Let me tell you something you already know." It's true, most motivational sayings are notions that deep down we already know—but in the throes of a challenge, are we always going to be able to access them? No. So it's important to keep mantras you can say to yourself in those moments when life has you knocked down in the ring, to remind yourself that in order to grow you must face your challenge, know your challenge, and embrace your challenge. The first step is to believe that you can use this challenge to grow. Notice the words. *You* can use this challenge—not this challenge will use you. You know this challenge. You know you will become stronger because of this challenge. You *own* this challenge. Once you own the challenge, it's no longer so daunting, because it's yours.

Sometimes the best way to own a challenge is to turn it from a negative to a positive. When I've had negative experiences in my life, my life coach has always asked me, "What is the blessing in this?" When you talk to people who have experienced a tragedy in their lives, they don't automatically think, "What is the blessing in this?" But those who thrive after a tragedy are able to find the blessing in what happened and by doing so are able to move forward. Those who never find the blessing stay rooted in the tragedy and are not able to move beyond their pain. They are not able to get back up from the hit.

There is an antidote for fear, and that is gratitude. If you fear falling off your bike, find gratitude for the opportunity to ride and the beauty of the day. If you fear people laughing at you because you are overweight, find a way to feel grateful that you are outside exercising. If you fear people looking down on you because of your monetary situation, find gratitude that you have a job and are contributing.

Sometimes you may need to turn to a professional who can guide you through the steps of overcoming your fear. A myriad of therapists, life coaches, and others specialize in helping others to identify their fear and make a plan to conquer it. Facing your fear will allow you to take action, and when you do so your fear will begin to diminish. Find a perspective that allows you to see your fear clearly.

When you look at your fear, understand that most fears stem from the feeling of failure. But failure is not the endgame. At the beginning of the chapter, we talked about how failure is but a step to your goals. Fear is a part of life that you can control, that you can change. Make the choice and face your fear.

Right now, think about what you fear. Take your fears out of the shadows and put them into the light. Everything is scarier if it's shrouded in darkness.

EXERCISE: Gratitude and Finding the Gift

Think of an athlete who has a career-ending injury. He cannot go back to his chosen profession. Now, what's the gift in this situation? Focus on the positive. He's alive—not six feet under. And all is not lost, because during his career he has mastered a certain skill set that not everyone has, and that is valuable to others. He can now take this skill set and share it with other people. He can become a coach and influence other people's lives and help them perform at their highest level.

To mimic this in your own life, at times when you need to find gratitude in a situation, try this exercise:

Write down what you want.

Next, write down why you want it. Focus on why, rather than how you are afraid to fail. By doing this you will see that everything in your life has a positive side. Your simple desire for something can be the positive, and so can the potential outcome. Once you set your plan into motion, even the task of trying to achieve it becomes a positive, because you are focusing on working toward a goal rather than on the fear of failure. When you are working toward something, every step you take is another step closer.

Look Forward, Never Backward

I heard a stand-up comic one evening who said, "You know, growing up we loved watching the Olympics. Every four years it was so exciting seeing the Olympics. These people who put in all this time and energy and to see what they accomplished in four to eight years. Then you turn thirty and all the Olympics does is remind you of all the crap you didn't do over the past four years and you feel like a failure."

As funny as that sounds, it's the truth. So many times we look back at our lives and all we see is failure. Don't look back. There's nothing there for you. We don't drive our cars backward to get where we're going. We don't sit backward in the classroom so we can't see the board. We have to look forward and ahead.

At the time of this writing, my niece Aspen loves gymnastics. She is eight years old and has dreams of winning a medal at the Olympics, like Shawn Johnson. On Aspen's wall is a chart showing all of Shawn Johnson's achievements and the age at which she accomplished them. She knows how many hours a week Shawn Johnson trained at her age and at what level she competed. By following Shawn Johnson's path to success, she has now made it her own path to success. She has taken ownership of the challenge.

Aspen currently practices twelve hours per week, and I have no doubt that by the time she has accomplished 10,000 hours of training she will succeed at her goal. If she were to add another eight hours to her weekly training, she would achieve 10,000 hours by the time she was seventeen. Only time will tell if she wins the gold medal, but I believe she can. Aspen knows that success leaves footprints.

A saying or mantra that I learned early on from a network marketing company is, "Find someone who has what you want. Do what they do, and you will get what they got!"

So ask yourself: Where do you want to be? What is your goal for the next four years? Once you've identified these goals, you can begin training and working like the Olympian you are. If you put in the work, you will achieve everything you want. To get there, you have to believe that anything is possible, because it is! Remember what Gabby Douglas, the little girl who grew up to be an Olympic gymnast, said: "You have to dream big." For so many people, the thought of anything being possible is "way out there." Beaten down by life, they simply stop believing. But not you!

Keep Going

Anyone who has ever run on a treadmill at high speed knows you get to a point where you feel like you can't go any further. That is the point where you turn up the music, you slap your face, you focus, you scream and yell to push through the pain, and you keep going.

Actor Will Smith, when asked once about the secret to his success said, "The only thing that I see that is distinctly different about me is I'm not afraid to die on a treadmill. I will not be outworked, period. You might have more talent than me, you might be smarter than me, you might be sexier than me, you might be all of those things you got it on me in nine categories. But if we get on the treadmill together, there's two things: You're getting off first, or I'm going to die. It's really that simple, right?"

It's really that simple. Right?

Chapter Four

MOTIVATION

There are only seven days in the week and "someday" is not one of them.

— Rita Chand —

L ET'S BEGIN this chapter with a simple question: What motivates you?

Before moving forward with a goal, the most important first step is to identify and understand what, if anything, is motivating you to achieve this goal. Many people assume that having a goal means that inherently, there is a valid motivation behind it. The hidden truth is that this may not be true.

For example, a person may have a goal of being a doctor. On the surface, this is a noble goal, right? However, let's think of two fictional residents in medical school. Sam wants to become a doctor because doctors make money, meaning right off the bat he is coming at it without sincere motivation. While he may accomplish the goal, his insincere motivation may come through in his practice, which is not a fulfilling outcome for Sam or for his patients. On the other side of the coin, Janet wants to become a doctor because as a child she had an illness and a doctor cured it, saving her life, and now she wants to save the lives of other people. Janet's not only going to be a doctor who will benefit thousands of people, she's also going to be doing it for the right reasons.

When young people who are in college or just starting out in their careers ask me, "Randy, what field should I go into? What should I do?" my answer is, "Find something that you love to do, something that you're passionate about. If you love snowboarding, then truthfully, go find some kind of occupation or work you can do that involves snowboarding. Because when you love it, it won't feel like work. If you can't identify why you want to do something, then cross it off your list and find out what it is that you do want."

Motivate Forward

Having a goal is about identifying a sincere motivator at the root; with change, it's more about being sincere about the outcome and simply moving toward it. When you decide to make a change, you may be acting out of desire or you may be acting out of desperation, but it really doesn't matter whether it's desire or desperation—something positive or something negative—that is leading you to make a change. The bottom line is, change is always forward movement. Whatever your motivation, as long as you are going in a forward motion toward a positive outcome, you are on the right track to achieving your goals. What is important is that you *make the change*.

What motivates a high school wrestler to spend four hours every single day training? That's what my high school wrestling coach Rob Ward had to figure out in order to be a great coach. He always asked us, "What turns you on? What gets you excited?" At the end of the day, what got me excited was to become the best me that I could possibly be. It wasn't about winning, it wasn't about accolades, it was about pushing myself as hard as I thought I could and then pushing even harder to become something or do something that I was previously unable to do. It was about the personal growth, that feeling I got inside, the confidence I found when I saw those results in the mirror. Asking us to figure out what personally motivated each of us made us all want to work hard to succeed.

At times, as I've said, change comes from the sheer fact that you are desperate. Desperation comes in many forms. You may be out of work and need money to pay your bills. Or, take one of my favorite teachers, who was about 150 pounds overweight. He was a great guy and everyone loved him. One day, he had a massive stroke and nearly died. His doctors told him, "If you don't change your lifestyle, you are going to die." That was his motivation. Whether his motivation was fear of death or not wanting to leave his loved ones, the point was that he chose to change his habits, because he wanted to live. He began to eat healthier foods, and every day he could be seen walking either alone or with his wife up and down the street. He chose to break his old bad habits and replace them with new ones, and while the initial cause for the change was negative, the outcome was very positive. The same can go for the example of needing more work in order to pay your bills. Although a negative situation is triggering this change, once you motivate forward, that momentum can lead to positive outcomes like finding a job, discovering new skills, becoming self-sufficient, and maybe eventually saving enough money to do something that turns you on and excites you, like traveling.

This brings us back to the essence of motivation. You have to find what "turns you on." What makes you want to get up in the morning and get to work? What do you think about at night? What can't you wait to work on tomorrow? What is the stuff of your dreams? You can have the life you want, the way you want it. It's all in your hands. Discover what "turns you on" and get to it. The thing to realize is that the end result is the goal.

EXERCISE: Know Your Motivation

For every situation, two people may find different motivation. For some, pain is a powerful motivator; for others it is desire. Each person and each situation is unique. What is important is to know that pain *is* a motivator. Too many people view pain as a stop sign in their lives. Pain and pleasure are both motivators.

CNN news anchor Anderson Cooper, a son of the Vanderbilt family and who is worth an estimated hundred million dollars not including any inheritance, had this to say about his motivation for success in an interview with Howard Stern on April 2, 2014: "My mom's made clear to me that there's no trust fund," he said. "There's none of that. Who's inherited a lot of money that has gone on to do things in their own life? From the time I was growing up, if I felt that there was some pot of gold waiting for me, I don't know that I would've been so motivated. [My mom has] made more money on her own than she ever inherited. We believe in working."

Cooper grew up aware that he wasn't going to receive an inheritance. So in order to continue the lifestyle he had as a child, he knew he had to be willing to work.

Now, take a look at what you desire and write it down. What is important in this exercise is to understand what you want. Understanding is the green light to achieving your goals. Now put to paper why you want this thing you desire—it may be an object like a couch, a lifestyle you want to maintain, or the simple ability to buy groceries for your children. Whatever it is, by doing this exercise you will be able to break down each step because you are aware of your motivation.

Sit in a quiet room and think about what you desire. See it clearly.

What are the steps to achieving this goal?

If there are things to overcome, what are the steps to overcome each hurdle?

How will you celebrate as you move toward your goal?

Envision your first step. See it clearly.

Then take the first step.

What's Most Important to You?

There are times when it's good to tune in and do a fact check on your life—to make certain that your goals are aligned with your values and the work you are putting in is moving you forward to what you want. You're not going to stay motivated for long if you lose sight of what's really important to you.

Ask yourself if what you are doing right now is the path to your success. Do you really live your life or do you go through the motions, assuming you will make changes another day? What if there weren't another day? What if this day were all you had? Are you the person you want to be? Have you achieved what's important to you?

Of the things you've thought of, what could you do today? What should you do today? When you look at it, the question becomes, why haven't you done these things? And what will it take for you to go do these things?

The ideas may be physical, like taking a trip around the world, or personal, like letting your family know how much you love them. Think and ponder your answers. How will you achieve these things and in what time?

Odds are, the things you would do on your last day are true to your core values. The emotions, ideas, and things that mean the most to you are what are most important in your life. Be happy in knowing you're now very aware of what the most important things are to you.

To put it in a nutshell, awareness is the most important part. You need to be aware of what you truly value, so that you can make those things the center of your plans and goals.

For instance, if you say that you value an amazing relationship with your partner or your kids, but you're working eighty hours a week, and when you get home you're so tired that you just want to sit in front of the TV and veg out—there's a disconnect there. If you can become aware and say, "Okay. Do I really value this? Is my behavior matching my value?" It may be that originally you had another goal of making a lot of money, which is why you're working eighty hours a week. When you become aware that what you really value now is that unbelievable relationship with your partner or kids, then perhaps it's time that the goal of making money should be modified so that you can spend that quality time with your loved ones.

Someday Never Comes

There are so many who wait for Someday. "Someday my prince will come" may work for the Disney princesses, but not so much in real life. Or, "Someday my ship will come in." Well, as the bumper sticker says, "Someday my ship will come in and I'll be at the airport." Likewise, "Someday I will win the lottery." Is that really a retirement plan?

You will see people all around you who constantly plan for something they never actually do. They plan for every single conceivable obstacle or dream, but they never get started. They think that Someday their plan will magically come together and they will be successful. As they wait for Someday, every day passes by, until yesterday is what they focus on. They focus on what they might have or should have done. They never live in the present. They never focus on what they can do today.

Perhaps those who wait for Someday really believe there is an eighth day they just haven't been able to access—an eighth day that exists for only a few, an eighth day no one has ever seen. This future Someday lives only in the imaginations of those who are not willing to roll up their sleeves and get to work, or those who are too scared to leave what has become normal for them, even if it's not what they want.

The hard truth is, Someday doesn't exist on any map or as an eighth day on any calendar. Someday is an excuse for not living your life. There is no clearer way to say it other than that *there is no Someday*. Someday is one of those "but" words. Someday I will be wealthy, *but* right now I'll go charge some furniture on my credit card. Someday I will be thin, *but* right now I'm having this banana split. Someday I will move to an island, *but* right now I will buy some electronic gadgets. Someday leads nowhere.

But there is good news: Today is your day. Today is your action day. Today is the day of your dreams. Everything you want begins today. Take *Someday* out of your vocabulary. Don't ever book a vacation for Someday. Don't ever set your goals for Someday. The only thing to do with Someday is to throw it out, today! There is a purpose in having a goal and working toward it, today. And you deserve and choose to be happy, right now, today.

It's true that it's not always easy getting away from Someday. Someday is a great excuse for not Doing It Now. Someday gets support from negative self-talk. Someday can be very loud when you are not focused. Someday can be strong when things aren't going your way.

But if you keep your focus on today, and adapt and reprioritize based on what you can and will achieve today, you will never look back in regret.

Someday is gone and Today is your day.

Today is the day you choose to move forward. Today is the day you are choosing to take the steps to your goal. You have no use for the nuances of life that take you from your path. You know what to do, and you will do it confidently and consistently, from today forward.

Chapter Five

CULTIVATING YOUR PERSONAL POWER

I am the greatest. I said that even before I knew I was.

— Muhammad Ali —

THERE COMES A POINT in your life when you hear your voice clearly. No matter what else is being said to you by others, you know the truth. You know the sound of your voice. Your voice will let you know if you are honoring yourself. Your voice will be louder than any others around. When that happens, you hold your personal power. You are powerful because you believe in yourself. You don't require others to telling you, because you believe it.

Just as having a strong, healthy body requires good nutrition and exercise, so does having a strong, healthy personal voice require affirmations, inspirations, and beliefs to feed it and keep it strengthened. The most important of these is believing in yourself. Your voice requires you to believe in it, so it has power. Without belief, you have no voice of your own.

Know Where You're Headed

There's not much difference between the psychology of being lost in the woods and being lost in life. Webster's dictionary defines lost as "unable to find the way." It's that way in life. People who are lost in life are unable to find the way. A large part of the reason we find ourselves in this condition is that we can't hear our own voice talking to us. We don't know what it is we really value or want in life. We're disconnected from our personal power and there's nothing driving us toward anything in particular.

People who are either lost in the woods or lost in life seldom take responsibility for the conditions they find themselves in. When lost in the woods, people say, "The trail wasn't clearly marked" or "I lost my compass." When lost in life, they say, "My boss fired me" or "I've been under a lot of stress." Either way it's an excuse, and in the end you got lost because of your own action or inaction. For example, if you never take the time to think about what's really important to you and how you're going to achieve your goals and dreams, that's inaction. If you do know, but you choose to take the easy way rather than the path you know will lead you to success because the latter is too difficult, that's an action, a choice you made, that will likely leave you lost in the wilderness of a directionless life.

When you're lost in life or lost in the woods, your perception of reality changes. It becomes distorted as you try to match your feelings with your reality. There are no clear paths to follow. There is nothing that leads you out—that's why you're lost. Everything looks the same, all the paths look the same, and there is no clear exit sign. You lose confidence in yourself. What was once familiar, no longer is. Your imagination takes over, and your memory is no longer certain. Panic sets in, and you are scared. You second-guess every decision, and nothing is clear.

Guess what? Every person has been lost sometime in his or her life. Every person has gotten turned around. There is no shame in getting lost. There are many reasons for getting lost. But in order to get out, you have to know your destination.

When Life Happens

My friends John and Alicia were the type who worked hard for everything they owned, choosing to be a two-income family, pay cash so as to avoid debt, and put their savings away for a rainy day on a regular basis. Well, that rainy day came in the form of a landslide that destroyed their home and many of the homes on their street. Their homeowner's policy did not cover this "act of God," and the bank didn't seem to care whether the house actually existed, demanding that they continue to pay on their home loan. They managed to find a small apartment, but their income was stretched to the max and they had lost most of their possessions. Every day they went to work, came home to the family, and wondered what would become of their life.

John and Alicia had once had a clear plan for their life together, but circumstances intervened and they certainly felt very lost. Finally, one night they pulled themselves out of their funk, sat down, and made a plan to get back on track to their new destination, which was to get out of debt and back into a home of their own. John took on another job, and with the additional income they were able to refinance the loan on the nonexistent house. They also decided, along with their neighbors, to file a lawsuit against the developer. After time, the developer settled and they had the money to rebuild. The additional money John was making from his second job replenished their rainy-day fund. It took them the better part of two years, but they found the way again.

Drifting Isn't as Nice as It Sounds

Imagine yourself getting into a raft and setting off down the Colorado River. You have no particular purpose in mind; you are just drifting along. Your general plan is to travel for three or four days. The first day is beautiful. The river winds through beautiful scenery, and you lean back and enjoy the ride. The second day you take out your fishing rod and throw a few lines into the water as you drift on by. Once again, it's a glorious day. The third day, you can feel the speed of the water picking up. As you look ahead, you notice that the water is churning. Hurriedly, you try to prepare for the turbulent water. You grab the handles of the raft and watch as your supplies are thrown out of the raft into the water, never to be seen again. By some miracle you survive the rapids and are able to get the raft to shore.

Once you get out of the raging water, you are thankful for anything solid. Then you realize that the GPS and all your provisions are gone. You and your raft are on a barren beach, with turbulent water all around, and you have no idea how you are going to get back. Then the questions come. Why did I ever think I could take this trip without planning? How could I make a decision without knowing anything about the river? So here you sit, on a beach, wondering if and when you are ever going to get back in the boat and head down the river.

What would ever make you think that drifting along would get you to your destination, especially if you didn't have one in mind? How would you know when you got there or whether you had even arrived? How would you know the path to an unknown goal?

You can and will get lost by just drifting along in life. If you don't take the time to listen to your own voice, if you have no idea of what you want and what you need, and have no goal in mind, you will get whatever comes your way. It's easy to fall into a drifting path. It's easy to just go along with the flow and not make decisions, not have goals. It's all easy until the Class 5 rapids come into play.

Being lost in life can come about by being pulled in so many directions that you don't take the time to focus on what you need to accomplish. You wander from thought to thought, task to task, job to job, never really going anywhere, just riding the flow. You don't care where you go, because you have no idea where you should be going. You can't hear that voice calling you, telling you that something is wrong. Or maybe it's trying to help show you the right way to go, but if you aren't listening, you'll just continue to wander.

The same theory applies in the workplace. If workers don't do the best job they can and just drift along, they and the company don't go very far. In fact, Workplace Options did a study in 2007 that found that distractions in the workplace cost American businesses about $650 billion dollars a year in lost productivity. That's a hefty price tag for distractions.

There are so many things that people identify as causing distractions, like constant cell phone alerts and the ever-present Internet. But the real reason you are distracted and lost is that you don't know where you're going. You have to focus on where you want to end up and how to get there. Without having a goal, without creating and planning a path and then doing it, you just drift from one distraction to another.

Have Some Confidence

In order to hear your voice, you have to be confident in yourself. The question is, "How do you build confidence in yourself?" Some athletes have addressed this question.

Jack Nicklaus said, "Confidence is believing in your own ability, knowing what you have to do to win. My confidence was developed through preparation." Jack Nicklaus's career spanned twenty years, and even today, he remains the inspiration for golfers like Tiger Woods.

Johnny Unitas, one of the greatest football quarterbacks in the game, said this: "I had complete confidence in my ability to carry out the game plan. I studied and accumulated knowledge of the game. I accomplished this in practice by practicing over and over again; hard work."

Both athletes said essentially the same two things. The first is that they believe they have the ability. They don't talk about how many shots they've missed or incomplete passes they've made; they talk about the fact that they have the ability. The second is that their confidence came from hard work. They worked hard and they practiced over and over and over.

You have the ability to succeed. You have the tools to enhance your ability. You have the desire to work hard, harder than anyone else. It's that desire that will propel you to success.

In high school, Anthony Robles won two state wrestling championships, going 96–0. He went on to win an NCAA championship, placing himself in a category of one of the most dangerous men in the world!

This feat alone is praiseworthy—especially if you consider that Anthony Robles was born with one leg. And on top of that, at age three, he decided he didn't want to use a prosthetic leg. Instead he learned to work around having one leg throughout his childhood. By the sixth grade he set the school record for the most push-ups, having gained strength in his arms by using his crutches. By the eighth grade he decided to wrestle after watching his cousins wrestle. In the ninth grade he was ranked last in his weight division, but he was only just beginning.

Anthony found that his lower center of gravity helped with defensive moves. He then created and perfected offensive moves using his unique skill set. With a strong spirit behind him, he trained tenaciously. He won the state championships in his junior and senior year of high school and culminated his senior year by being crowned the national champion in his weight class. He then went on to win the NCAA D1 wrestling championship in his senior year at Arizona State. In 2012 he was inducted into the National Wrestling Hall of Fame.

After winning the national championship he wrote a book, *Unstoppable*, and began a career in motivational speaking. He also garnered the Jimmy V Award at the ESPYs. When he received that honor he read a poem he'd written called "Unstoppable." This excerpt says it all: "I don't care what's probable, through blood, sweat, and tears, I am unstoppable."

Preparation = Self-Confidence

One of the greatest tennis players in history, Arthur Ashe, summed it up: "One important key to success is self-confidence. An important key to self-confidence is preparation."

Preparation is always a key ingredient for success. To this point, runners have an adage: "Nothing new on race day"—meaning, on race day, you take in the same nutrition and hydration, perform the same warm-up, and wear the same shoes and gear as during your training runs. But "nothing new on race day" applies to more than just runners.

Preparation is defined in Webster's dictionary as "the action or process of making something ready for use or service or of getting ready for some occasion, test, or duty." Preparation is always active. Self-confidence comes about when the individual knows she is capable of performing an act or action. That is where preparation comes in. By actively engaging in the preparation of having a certain skill set and achieving mastery of the skill set, a person knows she is capable and therefore self-confidence is activated.

Think about starting a business. Suppose you say, "I want to start a business selling flowers." That's great, but what's the plan? In order to believe this is possible you have to be prepared. You can start with writing an informal plan.

- What do you want to do?
- Why do you want to do it?
- How are you going to do it?

These are basic questions. Under each of these themes you break it down. For example:

- What do you want to do? (Sell flowers)
- What kind of flowers? (Bouquets)
- Where will you get your flowers? (I don't know)
- How much is your cost? (I need to find out)

The answers to each question require you to learn and activate a new skill set. As you find the answers to the questions, you have to be able take on the action required. For example, once you find out how much money you will need to start your business, then you need to make the preparations and undertake the necessary actions to get the money. Once the money is in hand, you will feel confident, because through your abilities you were able to get the money for your business. Confidence grows as each step of preparation is achieved. In conjunction with the actions you take and the successes you enjoy in the preparation stage, your self-confidence grows. By breaking down what you will need into small pieces, you can begin to see a plan taking shape. You will find the answers to the things you don't know. When you follow through in your preparation, you will face few new or unexpected challenges when you open your flower shop. You will be able to *Believe It* because you know what you are doing.

Being prepared can literally mean the difference between life and death.

In 2013, May Owen went for a climb on Mount Hood in Oregon. She fell the first day and cut her leg so badly that she couldn't walk off Mount Hood. She had to find a way to survive until someone came to rescue her.

Because she was an experienced hiker and climber, she was prepared. She built a snow cave, then had to adjust as the snowpack changed and small avalanches occurred. She had the tools to keep a fire burning, and she melted snow so she had drinking water. She didn't have a full pack of gear, but with her knowledge and skill set she found ways to survive. She was confident in her skills and knew she could survive until rescue arrived. With this knowledge she hunkered down and used her skills to stay optimistic.

Throughout it all, she maintained her faith that someone would come to her rescue. After six days, a National Guard helicopter spotted her and took her off the mountain. She had survived her ordeal because she was prepared, and her preparedness gave her the confidence to hang in there, rather than giving up.

Rethink Your Best

I had a coach who said, "Don't tell me you tried your best. You don't know what your best is." As a coach, he didn't want to coddle me and say, "It's okay. You tried your best."

You don't know what your best is. If you say, "I tried my best," all of a sudden you're in mediocrity and you get comfortable with saying, "I tried my best." The words my best are no longer true. They're just words without much meaning.

Entrepreneurs know this and use it to their advantage. Jennifer Adams, a successful interior designer, television personality on HGTV, and designer of home furnishings, listed four reasons for her success:

1. She has clear goals

2. She puts no restrictions on herself

3. She has a great team

4. She never stops learning

Her fourth reason, that she never stops learning, is a hallmark of success. Continuing to learn allows her to have no restrictions on her success. She knows that as long as she keeps learning, she is still working on doing her best.

Successful people know they are always capable of more. They choose to keep learning, and they never put a ceiling on how high they can go. They believe they can and will do more, and they do.

Everything that happened to you in the past, everything that is happening today, teaches you. Because you will never quit learning, never quit having experiences, good and bad, you will constantly be growing. Because you are constantly growing and never stopping, you have no idea what your best is.

Clear Your Funnel

Many people's thoughts focus on the negative. They dwell down deep and stay dark and angry. The problem with negativity is that it taints everything. Think of everything coming into your life as coming through a funnel. At the top, the area for things to enter is large. As they get ready to enter your life, the funnel narrows. Before anything new gets through, it must slow down and seep through what you already have in your funnel. If your funnel has positive energy, everything that passes through the funnel gains positive energy. If your funnel is clogged with negativity, even the best intentions become infected with negativity.

A positive outlook in life comes from having a clean funnel, and a negative attitude comes with having a dirty funnel, causing everything that comes into the funnel to be contaminated. It's pretty simple.

You might ask, how do I clean my funnel? It's not easy digging out all the negativity in your life. It has managed to push itself deep into a place where you will have to work to remove it. To get rid of it, you have to be willing to be honest about what you need to remove and then have the courage to remove it.

Take a clear look at your life and your thoughts. Be honest and really think about how you view your life, the areas that surround your life, the choices you make.

Next, decide which of these elements is negative. What makes them so? How do they affect your life? How are you responsible for the negativity happening—and sticking around?

After you determine your responsibility for the negativity, ask yourself how are you going to change what you can. What can you control in the situation that will make things better? It could be your thoughts, it could be stepping back and not engaging in a negative situation, it could be changing your hairstylist. Whatever it is, that is what you can control and change.

You now know what to do. You now know your part in the negativity, so now it is time to banish negativity from your life. That's where affirmations come in. Affirmations keep your funnel clean of negativity.

Affirmations are the way out of the cycle of negativity. Just as you visualize success, you also repeat it and hear it many times a day with affirmations. Affirmations feed your voice and shine a spotlight on believing it.

Transforming Thoughts into Tools

In a study at Ohio State University, researchers found that when people wrote down their thoughts on a piece of paper and then threw the paper away, they mentally discarded the thoughts as well.

On the other hand, people were more likely to use their thoughts when making judgments if they first wrote them down on a piece of paper and tucked the paper in a pocket to protect it.

"However you tag your thoughts—as trash or as worthy of protection—seems to make a difference in how you use those thoughts," said Richard Petty, coauthor of the study and professor of psychology at Ohio State University. "The findings suggest that people can treat their thoughts as material, concrete objects. That is evident in the language we use. . . . We talk about our thoughts as if we can visualize them. We hold our thoughts. We take stances on issues, we lean this way or that way. This all makes our thoughts more real to us."

So what does that mean for you? Actually, it means a lot. Writing your affirmations and keeping them in what you consider a safe place, be it your phone, your purse, or your wallet, will give your affirmations more power in your life. The more places you have them, the more times you read them, say them, sing them, get them in your head, the more real they become to you. That's what affirmations are about. They are about your reality. They add to your believing it.

Positive affirmations are one of the most powerful tools you have in your toolbox. Successful people, in business, in sports, and in life use them to strengthen their voice and their beliefs. Notice the word *positive*. Affirmations are always in the positive, without any hint of negativity.

The late Dorothy Harris, PhD, a professor of sports psychology at Pennsylvania State University in University Park, used to say, "The only difference between the best performance and the worst performance is the variation in our self-talk and the self-thoughts and attitudes we carry around with us."

Dr. Harris used this philosophy in her battle with pancreatic cancer. When her doctors gave her the news of her cancer and prognosis, she said she would outlive their prognosis by one year. She outlived their prognosis by two years through the use of visualization and positive affirmations. Even in the face of impending death, she chose to believe she would live longer than the experts said she would. She understood the power of affirmations and visualization, in sports and in life.

Affirmations are so important to me that I keep them with me all the time. I keep my affirmations safe in my iPhone, and I've actually programmed my phone to pop up my affirmations. I've written my affirmations to include "Think abundance, feel abundance, see abundance. Believe abundance. Unlimited health, success, happiness, and strength." These are my basic affirmations that stay constant. After those, I list some of the things I'm working toward in my life.

Affirmations are used to block out negative past experiences. So many of our present actions are based on the results of past experiences. It can be as simple as this: The last time you washed the floor you slipped and fell. The next time you wash the floor, you are afraid you're going to slip, you focus on that thought, and inevitably you fall. Affirmation and strong self-talk empowers you to get around those negativities of the past and focus on the positive potential of the future.

Writing Your Own Affirmations

When you use affirmations, they are for you and no one else. They are there to strengthen your belief, fuel your voice, and bring great things to you. When you write affirmations, think of the things you will achieve or want to have in your life.

Affirmations are personal. They only have to be about you and what you desire, what you believe, who you are. Writing affirmations is one of the times in life when it's to your advantage to be selfish. You can't write affirmations for someone else, only yourself.

The easiest way to start is with this phrase: *I am.* For example, *I am healthy. I am happy. I am in great shape.* Write your affirmations as though you already have those things. Do not use the words *I want* or *I need.* Those are not positive thoughts. Start with *I am.* For example, if you want to have a healthy relationship, you could write, "I am in a healthy relationship that fulfills me unconditionally."

Using *I am* won't always work; there are other words such as *I have*, *I feel*, and *I love* that you can use because they are in the present.

The word *affirmation* comes from the word *affirm*, which is defined as "to state as a fact or declare one's support for." With that in mind, all affirmations are written in the positive and in the present. By writing the affirmation, by saying the affirmation, you are deciding it is a *fact* of your life, not a wish, and that you support having it in your life.

So, if you are looking to lose weight, the affirmation can say, "I am at a healthy body weight of 170 pounds." It shouldn't read, "I will lose weight." See the difference? The first statement, "I am at a healthy body weight of 170 pounds," states that at this moment in time you are at your healthy body weight. The second, "I will lose weight," means you have not achieved your goal. Write your affirmations as though they have already been achieved. Write them in the now, not in the future.

Because you write your own affirmations, they should be passionate and personal. Consider the first weight loss affirmation, "I am at a healthy body weight of 170 pounds." Now you can add how you feel: "I am at a healthy body weight of 170 pounds, and I feel energetic." Adding your feelings makes the affirmation more real to you.

Affirmations also apply to things you have in the present. If you are at ideal body weight, your affirmation could be, "I am fit and healthy with 12 percent body fat." Many of my affirmations refer to things that are already in my life. When you have achieved something, you still have to care for it. You still have to affirm that it's what you want so you don't lose focus.

Affirmations need to be in your voice and to the point, with words you familiarly use. You are writing them for yourself, so they have to ring true to you. Affirmations are the words that change how you think. They are powerful because they have the power to change how you see yourself.

You have to be able to remember your affirmations and commit them to memory. Think of your affirmations as being tweets you send to yourself. Not only will you write them down and keep them safe, you will also keep them safe in your memory to repeat as a mantra numerous times throughout the day, whenever you need reassurance.

There will be times when you are going to have to repeat your affirmations and they may not be at hand to read. If you're losing weight and your friends stop by the Cheesecake Factory for dessert after you've all been out to dinner, you should be able to quickly recall your affirmation of "I eat healthy and nutritious foods" so you don't cave and order that extra-large piece of praline cheesecake.

If you're in the mall and the cream-colored sofa in the window is calling out to you, recall your affirmation, "I follow my budget and am growing richer by the day." By repeating that, you will cause the couch to lose its pull on you, keep your money, and achieve your desired goal.

EXERCISE: Experimenting with Affirmations

Who is the person you brush your teeth with? For some of you it may be a spouse or a child, but most of you probably brush your teeth by yourself. During the time you spend brushing your teeth, take the time to encourage yourself. Unless you have ventriloquism skills, I don't believe that saying affirmations out loud while you're brushing your teeth would be the right thing. But when you're done, start the day with your affirmations. Write them down on slips of paper and tape them to your bathroom mirror. Read them out loud and with energy. The reason I suggest tooth-brushing time is that it's something you do every day. Because brushing your teeth is already a habit, pairing it with saying your affirmations first thing every day creates another good habit.

Here's a great affirmation to experiment with: "Every day, in every way, I am getting better and better."

Once you're in the habit, you can try incorporating affirmations more specific to your goals. We'll talk more about this in the workbook.

Forgive Yourself, Forgive Others

Chris Williams is a man who has been both the recipient of and the giver of forgiveness.

When Chris was sixteen years old, a little boy ran in front of his car and was instantly killed. Chris's memories of that night revolve around sitting in the back of a patrol car and trying not to fall apart. It was a horrible accident that seemed to freeze time, but as Chris's life slowly continued forward, he understood that he had to learn to forgive himself. And he did. Many years later, when Chris became a father, he often thought about that young boy and remembered how life can change in an instant. He incorporated that thought into his life on a daily basis.

On February 9, 2007, Chris again experienced this powerful lesson. As he and his family were driving home after having dessert out together, a seventeen-year-old boy's car collided head-on with theirs. Instantly Chris's wife and two of his three children were killed. Chris and his third child were badly injured.

From his shattered window, Chris could see that the other car involved in the accident had overturned. At that moment, a moment eerily familiar, he decided to forgive the other driver. Without knowing the circumstances, without knowing the person behind the overturned car's wheel, his first thought became, "Let it go."

This act of forgiveness was not easy. During the next few years of his life, Chris wrestled with anger and resentment, but in every case, his thoughts always returned to "Let it go." Two years after the accident, he met the driver of the other car. The young man asked questions about how Chris's life had changed and wanted to know more about the people he'd killed that night. Chris found peace in that meeting, and from that day on he never viewed the other driver as "the guy who killed my family," but as someone who simply needed forgiveness. Just as he had needed it once a long time ago.

Through all of the pain and anger Chris learned to forgive, let the hurt go, move on with his life, and heal. That's how it works. Once forgiveness takes hold, the rest will fall into place. Showing forgiveness to yourself and others is the final step in being happy. No one is perfect. No one is blameless. What people forget is that by making mistakes, even horrible ones, they are learning. By learning, they are growing. It doesn't matter what mistakes you've made in the past—you deserve to forgive yourself.

Only once you forgive yourself can you truly forgive others. Forgiveness is the greatest gift you can give to others and to yourself. By forgiving, you let go of the pain, you let go of the resentment, but you keep what you learned from the experience.

One of the hardest parts of forgiving is forgiving everything that needs to be forgiven. So it's important to remember when forgiving that you make sure to clean your funnel. Make certain that you forgive every part of what needs to be forgiven. If you only forgive certain things and not others, you allow the negativity to clog your funnel. With a clean funnel, you can move on to a happier, clearer horizon.

Choose Your Own Label

Many people in this world are labeled victims by others. It doesn't matter what someone else labels you, because only you have the right to label yourself. Stop accepting labels from others, and never, ever label yourself. You are so much more than just a label. You are never a victim. You always choose how you act, how you respond, and how you believe. Everything in your life ultimately is your choice; it is your choice how you perceive it and how you act on it.

There are times when people can choose to look at themselves as victims. Those who choose to be victims waste their lives in pitying themselves. Then there are those who do more than survive, and choose to thrive. Regardless of the situation, regardless of where they are in a particular moment, they choose success. They believe they deserve success, and ultimately they achieve success.

Victimization happens every day, in every culture, in every age group. Everyone will have numerous opportunities in life to either lie down and be a victim or choose to make the bad times meaningful and use them for strength. Indeed, there are people who are true victims, but so many of these victims choose to build successful and meaningful lives. They look past what happened and move on to their future, to what they can control, and they are able to let go of the things they can't control.

When your first reaction to a situation is to point your finger at someone or blame someone, anyone, in the vicinity, for the outcome, then you are acting the victim. You choose to blame someone else for the outcome. That is being a victim. Things happen that aren't good. Things happen that don't go your way. You need to take action when things are different than you'd hoped.

The second you take action, your role as victim is gone. You are now responsible for what's happening around you, and most importantly you are responsible for how you act and feel.

And there's a great thing that happens when you're no longer a victim: your confidence rises. Thoughts become encouraging. Self-talk takes on a new, positive tone. Rather than continuing in the downward spiral of victimization, you begin to rise. With every action, every thought, you move upward.

When you are no longer the victim, when you change, your world will change along with you. You *Believe It*, and the world believes with you.

Leave the Pity Party

You might say, "I'm not a victim. I know the difference. There's just some things in my life that are tough." Okay, but the question you need to ask is, "How do I deal with the tough stuff?" Do you complain? Or do you feel sorry for yourself? If so, are these responses to a specific moment in time or do they influence your life in a more long-term sense? If the answer is that they last longer than a very short period, you are acting as a passive victim. You are letting circumstances control your life, rather than taking charge and living the life you desire, the life you believe you can have.

There are a myriad of ways to be a victim. Much of the way we victimize ourselves is through self-talk: telling ourselves things like, "I lost my job," "I'm too fat to work out," "I can't have kids," "I'm not married," and on and on. To put a stop to this negative spiral, keep in mind that whenever you choose to indulge yourself in self-pity, you willingly take on the role of the victim. Anyone and everyone has something they can complain about. There are things that happen to people that are not fair, and they can be devastating. But they only gain more power, more momentum when you don't take charge. It's hard to take charge when things are out of control, so take charge of what you can, *now*!

There are times in your life when you need to lick your wounds like a hurt animal. That is a short-term solution. During that time, you can build up some defenses; you can arm yourself with the emotional tools you will need to fight your way out of victimization—but remember something about animals licking their wounds. It's okay for a few days, but if they don't stop, the wound will become infected and eventually the animal will die.

If you hear yourself complaining, *STOP IT!* Instead, ask yourself how you fit into the picture. Ask yourself, "Why is this happening to me?" Then ask yourself, "How am I going to work on the part of the problem that is mine?" Once you do that, you are no longer a victim. Once you take control in of your part, then and only then can you move out of victimhood and into your life.

The Serenity Prayer, written in about 1936, is recited by hundreds of thousands of people every single day for different reasons. Regardless of why it is said, in its simplicity it brings comfort.

The Serenity Prayer

God grant me the serenity to accept the things I cannot change;

the courage to change the things I can;

and the wisdom to know the difference.

This thought has been around for hundreds of years. The eleventh-century Jewish philosopher Solomon ibn Gabirol wrote:

At the head of all understanding—is realizing what is and what cannot be, and the consoling of what is not in our power to change.

The Indian Buddhist scholar Shantideva of Nalanda University wrote:

If there's a remedy when trouble strikes,

What reason is there for dejection?

And if there is no help for it,

What use is there in being glum?

For centuries humankind has dealt with feelings of victimization. It flows throughout cultures and times. It can be overcome.

To begin overcoming, try this exercise: List everything in your life that's good. Remember that no matter how bad you feel, there is something to be grateful for. Watch for acts of random kindness. If you do, you will see them every day. Perform an act of random kindness. Make certain that your actions are those you can be proud of, not ones that pull you down.

Your Life Isn't as Bad as You Think

Barry had been happily married for fifteen years. He thought his marriage was solid and his future life secure. Then one day, his wife announced that she wanted a divorce, because she had fallen in love with another man.

Barry was devastated. Suddenly all his plans for the future vanished with the signing of the divorce papers. His happiness, his financial fitness, everything was falling down the rabbit hole. His whole road map of what he thought life was supposed to be just fell apart and took him to a deep, dark place. He became very depressed and because of that, he lost his job—a very well-paying job with a salary of over two hundred thousand dollars a year. He was just too depressed to keep working. So he decided to seek professional counseling.

For the next few months, he continued to wallow in his pain. Every therapy session was the same. Even worse, he displayed the same attitude with his friends and family. Slowly, one by one, his friends pulled away. His family was no longer at his beck and call. This only added to his sad-sack demeanor. By the end of six months, he remained the victim, still wasn't working, and had moved into his mom's basement. To add to that, he had put on about forty pounds and had stopped taking care of himself and his physical appearance. Victimized by himself and his feelings, he existed in the constant state of emotional pain he'd created.

His kid had tried to help, his family had tried to help, but it wasn't until his therapist asked him for a favor and said, "Can you please go and teach this class at the women's prison?" that things started to turn around. His therapist had advised him to do something for someone else, so one day he decided to go ahead with it, and he went down to the prison.

When Barry walked into the prison, he walked in with the mentality of a victim, but it soon became clear that the women in prison had things much worse than he did.

He met a women who told him her story. "My husband had a real bad drug problem. When he got high he beat me and the kids. I could take what he did to me, but when he threw our two-year-old through a door I snapped. I stabbed him with a kitchen knife and killed him. I got locked up, lost my rights to my kids, and now I'm alone."

Barry realized that his life wasn't at the bottom of the deck. His life was pretty good, and he made a choice to live his life, no longer playing the victim card.

When he tried focusing on himself, nothing helped. It wasn't until he gave himself and was freely offering service at the women's prison that he found purpose—and thought, "I can actually help someone else." From there he had a feeling of purpose and started to have a glimmer of hope. He shaved, he started working again, and he started making money.

To make a happy ending even happier, Barry also started going back to the gym, where he met someone, and they started dating. Not only that, but he kept losing the weight, kept working on himself, and now he and the woman he met at the gym are married. And even after that, he continued to go to the prison because that was where he felt like he was creating value for other people, and that made him feel good about himself.

From there, Barry could see his choices more clearly. He realized he had the choice and the power to make his world better. He had the power to live the life he wanted. He no longer remained a victim, waiting passively for things to get better.

EXERCISE: Help Someone Else to Help Yourself

Self-pity has one very frightening component: It's self-perpetuating. That is, if you continue to wallow in your pity, you feed on it, and it grows even bigger. In order to stop self-pitying, you have to stop. Yes, that sounds odd, but there's no other way to say it. Just stop! Find a way to help others.

No Buts Allowed

Once you believe in yourself, all things become possible. However, there is always one potential problem lurking around. It's the *but*. The best of us have to deal with the ever-present *but*. Whatever it's in regard to, this categorized *but* will try to change your life if you allow it. It will sneak into your mind and create havoc.

But is a powerful word, much more powerful than its three letters indicate. It can derail the best of intentions; it can cause affirmations to waver.

To get past the *but*s, let's start by discussing how affirmations work. As you continue to think and say your affirmations, your unconscious mind will begin to determine whether it believes them. The more you repeat them, the more your subconscious will tune in to them, and eventually it will accept the affirmations as the truth. When that occurs, you will know it. Your affirmations will seem truer. Your entire thought process will shift to your belief. How you think and feel about things in your life will change. Your life will change to fit what you believe.

In *Feeling Good: The New Mood Therapy Revised and Updated*, Dr. David Burns says, "*but* may be our biggest obstacle to effective action."

But is such a small word that its power is often overlooked. For example, if your affirmation is, "I eat healthy and nutritious food," *but* can sneak in. "I eat healthy and nutritious foods, *but* I'm at the fair and everyone else is having a corn dog." Or "I eat healthy and nutritious foods, *but* it's Grandma's birthday and it's not my fault she ordered chocolate cake."

For such a small word, *but* holds the power of a neutron bomb. From now on, you need to be aware of the *but*s in your life. They are not there to help you achieve your goals; rather, they are the landmines designed to divert you from your path to success. *But* is not a word that should be in your vocabulary. It's a word for victims or people who do not *Believe It*.

There are a myriad of exercises you can do to convince yourself that *but* isn't a good choice. You can write down the *but*, followed by writing why it's either positive or negative. At some point you will come to a conclusion on the particular *but* you're dealing with. But as a general rule, *but*s are not going to be justified.

Let's take the preceding example from above—"I eat healthy and nutritious foods *but* I'm at the fair and everyone else is having a corn dog." The following is the give and take of essentially what might be going through your mind:

"If I choose to eat the corn dog, I will feel happy"

followed by

"I may or may not feel guilty that I broke my affirmation"

In this situation ask yourself: Purpose or pleasure?

It's okay to eat for pleasure, if you aware of what you are doing and the effect it will have on you. The next thought process might be:

"If I feel guilty, my guilt will only last for a little while"

followed by

"Okay, maybe I shouldn't bother trying to lose weight" Or: "I will eat the corn dog *and* I will go for a two-mile run to burn off the extra calories"

This is the case of the *but*s. In the end, you will see that all the *but* did was attempt to derail you from your goal. It's a sneaky little word; if you don't immediately reject it, it will bring baggage and find more and more ways to creep into your life, into your affirmations, and into your beliefs.

In these cases the simple answer is, you're usually better off leaving the whole *But* family off the contact list of your life. To do that, try writing down your *but* lists each time something comes up to derail you from an affirmation, until you are so used to the exercise that you can do it in your head. After all, many decisions in life are made on the fly, and you can't always stop in the middle of a carnival to take notes!

Chapter Six

TAKING OWNERSHIP

What is necessary to change a person is to change his awareness of himself.

— ABRAHAM MASLOW —

YOU ALONE are the master of your life. There are no limits to what you can and will achieve, other than those you set. You have gifts, and you have the ability to master any skill or talent with hard work. Don't look around at others with envy or even a whisper of dismissing the amazing you. Your talents, your skills are valuable. They are the path to achieving what you desire.

Remember that every single thing you focus on will grow in your life, so it's important to set your focus on the skills and the talents that will propel you forward. Never settle for what is just likely; focus on the limitless potential in your life. *Likely* is for people who don't believe they can have everything in life. You are different. You believe you can have everything you want, because you know you can work for it. Everything in the world is possible for you. Everything.

Whatever stage of belief you're in, right now is a good time to stop, accept, and own the power inside you. You need to be aware that you can do anything and have anything you want. To do this, you just have to want something as badly as you want to breathe. Whatever happened in the past doesn't stop you from moving forward today. In fact, the past can be the reason you move forward today. There is a lesson in every action, in every consequence. The past has given you lessons, and when you use them in a positive way, the past propels you forward.

Everyone has something in the past that they wish they could forget or change. Remember Chris Williams from the previous chapter: If he could forgive himself for accidentally killing a child, if he could forgive another young man for killing his own children and his wife, then so can you find forgiveness for the wrongs in your life. And you must. Instead of using the past as a roadblock, try using it as fuel for your present. Learn from those past actions, embrace them, and own them. Once you do, they have no power over you. You now own all your power. You own your life and you can have anything you want; you just have to work for it.

Don't settle. Don't be a person who looks back at the past and says, "That was the best time in my life." The best time in your life is yet to come. The only limitation you have is yourself. The only limitation you see is one you choose to see. The only limitation you hear is what you choose to hear. The only limitation you speak is what you choose to speak.

It's All Your Fault

Aside from when you're a true victim of outside circumstances, everything in your life is your own damn fault. The first thing you have to do is accept this. If you're happy, it's your fault. If you're healthy, successful, in a great relationship with your spouse and kids, it's your fault—because of the actions you have taken. If you're overweight, miserable, have a horrible relationship with your spouse, with your parents, with your children—it's you. Look in the mirror and take ownership of that. That's the first step.

Acknowledge that you are where you are because of your decisions and the things you've done. This may seem like a downer, but taking ownership is a positive step. Taking ownership of your problems just put you on the road to changing your life! If you don't take ownership, you have no desire to change, because you blame someone else. Once you realize this and take responsibility, you have the power to have anything you want. You just have to *Believe It* and work for it.

It's very helpful to keep your focus on how to solve a problem or get something good out of a current situation, rather than ask yourself "why?" over and over and thereby focus on making yourself feel worse and worse. Once you begin the descent into Poor Pitiful Me Syndrome, it's hard to see anything else. When all you do is look down, you can never see the sun. Look up! Look around you. See the entire situation. Discover where you fit in.

You can control how you choose to act in a situation. The situation is never in control of how you act or how you feel. Those are things that belong solely to you. When you choose to let circumstances, events, or people define you, it's your fault. Only you can choose to give your power away. Starting today, take ownership of your power and make the decision not to give it away.

You Can, You Will

According to an article at Examiner.com, "Kathy Buckley almost died at birth. She had aseptic meningitis at age five; during her childhood, she was sexually abused. As a young adult she had two serious car accidents. Then one day, while sunbathing on a beach, she was run over by a jeep and her body was crushed. During the next few years, she suffered from debilitating seizures. Later, she was stricken with malignant cancer. Did I forget to mention she also has hearing loss that went undiagnosed until she was eight years old? People had thought she had a mental deficiency. Unable to hear the people around her, she quickly learned how to read lips, all the while desperately trying to fit in. Over and over, the message she received from others was: "You can't, you won't, you're ugly, you're broken, you're stupid."

Now that's a tough life. How many of you have faced as many adversities as Kathy Buckley? How many of you have felt victimized by fewer traumas than Kathy Buckley has endured throughout her life? Yet Kathy Buckley does not believe she is a victim. In fact, she says, "All my challenges have been a blessing put on me. There's a reason I went through everything I did, so I could be a tool to help others."

Before you say, "You've got to be making this up. A person couldn't possibly have gone through all that and come out smiling," I should tell you there was a time in Kathy Buckley's life when she was angry, very angry. At one point in her life, she was full of bitterness and resentment. She now looks for the humor in her childhood experiences, but for years, her hardships were no laughing matter. Then slowly, she came to this belief: "My thoughts and words had become my enemy. My limitation, my disability was of my own making."

Today, Kathy Buckley works with children who have hearing loss. She helps the parents understand their children's lives, because her parents had always chosen to ignore her hearing loss. In addition to her work with children, Kathy Buckley is also a motivational speaker. You can see that there are no limits in her life. She believes in herself. Today, Kathy's words are, "You can, you will, you're beautiful, you're unbroken, you're intelligent."

Kathy Buckley made a choice, a choice to own her power, a choice to believe. And a choice to give her message to others with a dose of humor, because she is also a comedian. Her message is delivered in many ways, and she sums up her life's work:

"I want people to know that they can choose to live, not just exist. No matter how hard their life has been or how they have been treated, they are worthy of all the good things the world has to offer. But it has to be their choice to focus on the good things and let go of the bad."

Now think about your hardships. Think about how you approach your life. Have you learned anything? If you have, what are you going to do about it in a positive way?

EXERCISE: Gaining Perspective

I want you to think about your life. Think about your challenges and how they have weighed you down in the past, or even how they continue to do so now. Take a couple of minutes to remember them and how you felt or feel. How do you think your life compares to that of others? Are you more or less fortunate? Do you believe your life is good or bad? Got the answers? Now read on.

Awareness

How do you become aware of your situation? How do you find a way to identify where you are right now? Look around you and focus on being aware of your situation and of everything in your life. You may not see everything clearly right now, but you will. You will be able to make choices. It's okay to make mistakes, as long as you are aware of the reality.

Here's one example that's closer to my own life: Sweet Arlene's. Sweet Arlene's makes the best red velvet cupcakes. If you haven't eaten one, you haven't lived. But if you're trying to watch your weight, a cupcake poses a situation that requires awareness. You have to be aware that if you eat a cupcake, you will have to make up for it by working out more and/or eating less of something else. It is your choice to eat the cupcake and your choice to work out more because you ate one. Choices are never mistakes when you're aware. It's the act of making choices or decisions without awareness that has no value.

One of my favorite apps is called Lose It! This app will track everything I consume and all of my activity. When I track what I eat, I'm aware of it and recognize what I'm doing. If I consume more calories than I use, then everything over what I use up turns to fat. It's that simple. I choose to eat what I want, knowing what the consequence is and how I can balance the scale with more exercise or fewer calories somewhere else.

When being aware, you have to realize that "you don't know what you don't know." You have to internalize the thought and understand it. Simply by virtue of knowing that "you don't know what you don't know," you are no longer ignorant. Awareness brings you power. The ability to keep your mind open to more information gives you the power to learn and integrate what you learn into your life.

I have a coworker who was always spilling something on his shirt. When we went to lunch, he'd get mustard, soy sauce, something on his shirt every single time. He said this had been going on for years, and he'd just accepted it. My response was, "Hang on a second—let me talk you through this. It's a matter of being aware of what you're doing. You're shoving food in your mouth like George Costanza from *Seinfeld*. Slow down. Take a bite, lean over your plate if you have to, get a napkin. Be aware of what you're doing when you take a bite. If you're aware, the chances of you spilling something on your shirt go down dramatically."

I'd forgotten about that story, but about a month later he said, "Randy, you'd be so proud of me! I haven't spilled anything on my shirt for a month." I'm not surprised. As I said, it's about awareness—about you being aware of your actions.

Self-Awareness

But wait! There's more to awareness than just what is going on around you. You need to be aware of yourself: your strengths, your weaknesses, where you thrive, and where you struggle. Self-awareness has many aspects that affect your everyday living and your experiences. Being aware of your strengths doesn't mean that's all you have. It just means you are beginning further down the track than some others. You can master any skill, but you should also realize your strengths and capitalize on them.

You need to be aware of your personality. If you are an extremely shy person, having a job in cold sales wouldn't suit you, unless you choose to master the skills necessary for that job. You can master the skills, you just need the awareness that you will need to work hard to accomplish them. Being aware of your personality will propel you forward.

Consider Joan, a woman who once worked for one of my companies. After several years of good service as a receptionist, Joan's supervisor suggested that she might be ready for something more, and so we promoted her to customer service. Her salary increased, as did her value to the company. She interviewed very well for the promoted position, and her supervisors felt optimistic that she'd carry out the new job very well.

Day after day, Joan's job entailed listening to complaints from customers and trying to find solutions, or at least resolutions, to the complaints. Unfortunately, Joan didn't have the skill of listening. She didn't have the skill of patience, and she didn't have the skill of flexibility. Most importantly, she didn't have any desire to master these skills, and at one point, she made a customer on the phone very upset by speaking in a condescending manner. When her supervisor approached her about it, she showed no sign of acknowledging that she had done anything wrong. When her supervisor offered her training, she declined. When her supervisor asked her to read and listen to some information on how to hear what others are saying, she declined. Eventually Joan was fired.

To be successful in many situations, both personal and professional, you need to be aware of your emotions. Understanding how you react or don't react to a situation is part of your self-awareness. Different jobs in life, like the positions on a sports team, require different sets of skills—skills you need to be aware of, skills you can master, *if* you are aware of them.

For instance, being a goalkeeper on a soccer team is very different than being a player on the field. Shep Messing, lead analyst for the New York Red Bulls and former goalkeeper, explains, "All goalkeepers belong to a fraternity of renegades. Goalkeeping is intensely psychological. For ninety minutes, you are on the precipice of anger and tranquility. You have to be coiled and ready to strike, and at the same time have the serenity of a yogi."

Learning about the skills of a goalkeeper is imperative if you want to be a goalkeeper. It doesn't mean you can't be a goalkeeper if you don't already have those skills; it simply means you need to learn the skills that a goalkeeper needs to be one. You have to be aware of your emotions in order to learn the skills required. You have to know what to work on, what might initially be easier or harder for you. But remember, it doesn't matter if it's easy or difficult; what matters is how hard you work at it.

Being aware doesn't mean you can't have what you want. Being aware is a key step toward clarifying what you want and creating a plan to get it.

Revisit your habits. To be aware of who you are, you need to understand and control your habits. Think about who or what is in charge of your life; is it you, or is it your habits? It's scary to think that something you do every day, without thinking, may be the reason you are where you are. Take stock of your habits and note the ones you want to change—then start changing them. Your habits have control only when you give it to them. Empower yourself. You have the power to be whoever you want, to have whatever you want, to make the changes you want. You are in control of your own life. The power you have inside you propels you toward more in your life. Every time you give away your power, you suffer. Take all your power back, right now!

When You Need Help

When you know which beliefs are hurting you, it's time to take action and get help. Sometimes that means personal help, and sometimes it means professional help. If you're suffering from low self-esteem or self-doubt, then you may need a professional. You need to work with people who can help you overcome your challenges. There are people who have experience with the challenges you face, and their knowledge will accelerate you toward your goals.

Reaching out for help is the sign of a *strong person*. So many people try to do it on their own, feeling that they are weak if they ask for help. Being humble enough to ask for help when you need it is one of the first signs of strength. It may sound strange to say that asking for help shows strength, but it does.

The more resistant you are to asking for help, the more stress you put yourself under, and the harder it feels to receive help from anyone. To start helping yourself, admitting your imperfections is one of the first things you need to do. No one's life is perfect. No one has everything in the right place at the right time all the time. One of the most limiting beliefs anyone can have is that they can stand alone, without the help of anyone. Admit that you are not alone, and that there are people who can help you.

You Reap What You Sow

The saying "You reap what you sow" has its beginnings in religious writings such as the Bible and the Qur'an. In the Bible it can be found in numerous passages, but it is very clear here:

Galatians 6:7 (King James Version)
Whatsoever a man soweth, that shall he also reap.

In the Quran it appears as follows:
Qur'an 17:7

If you do good, you do good to yourselves. [Likewise,] If you do evil, you do evil to yourselves.

In Buddhist scripture, the Samyutta Nikaya expands on the idea:

Kindred Sayings, Part 1

According to the seed that's sown,

So is the fruit you reap there from,

Doer of good will gather good,

Doer of evil, evil reaps,

Down is the seed and thou shalt taste

The fruit thereof.

This idea is paraphrased in almost all religious books and is a universal principle; the idea that "you reap what you sow" is true for everyone in all times and places.

A farmer lives or dies by the Law of the Harvest and literally reaps what is sown. Beginning with a piece of land overgrown with weeds and rocks, he says to himself, "I can grow corn here. The weeds are thriving, so it must be good soil, and I have a water source. I will turn this piece of land into a cornfield."

That day he cuts down the weeds and painstakingly removes all the rocks from the field so he can plow. Once he plows, more rocks turn up and again he removes them from the plowed field. He cultivates the soil, puts in some fertilizer, and then plants the seed. Every day he goes to the field and waters every seedling and later every plant. Once the corn stalks are tall, he harvests the corn and fills his corn bin. Every action he performed, every rock he removed from the field, was worth it, as now his corn bin is full.

The Law of the Harvest

There are no shortcuts; there are no quick fixes. To get the best results, you have to put in the work.

EXERCISE: The Law of the Harvest

What are you sowing in your life right now? Stop and think about what you did today. Remember that every action has a consequence, good or bad. To enjoy the benefits of the harvest you must choose positive actions to receive positive consequences. Think about what you ate, who you interacted with, what activities you did. If you need prompts, try questions like these:

- How did you treat your family?
- How did you treat your coworkers?
- How did you treat your body?
- How did you further your education?

Write down everything you did on the left side of a piece of paper. On the right side, write down whether your action will bring you rewards, and what those rewards are. If the consequences of your actions are not positive, stop and write down how you are going to change the action, and then DO IT!

For example:

ACTION	CONSEQUENCE OF ACTION
Told spouse I love her	Better relationship with wife
Had an extra-large milkshake	Blood sugar elevated—no health benefits
CHANGE: Drink water	Blood sugar stable—getting healthier

Choose to Respond, Not React

Julia is one of those people who are always late: the person you invite to a party an hour early because she'll show up an hour late. This irritated her family and frustrated her friends. What was even worse was that it was always the same kind of excuse. "I had to take a call" or "I was answering my e-mail." Her closest friends finally decided they wouldn't wait anymore. They still invited her to join them for lunch, and inevitably they were finished and gone before she got there. This happened twice before she got the idea. The third time she showed up on time, and they had a pleasant lunch.

> It might sound like Julia learned her lesson. It's true that Julia learned to be on time—but the other lesson was that her friends learned not to wait for her. They learned to not be distracted by Julia's actions. It would have been easy to blame the fact that they waited on Julia, but in truth they waited because they chose to wait. Once they chose to move on, they were free from distraction.

Gain Control and Don't Let Go

Darlene worked for a boss who was very demanding and always placed the blame on Darlene if something wasn't right. Darlene took the blame and in time began to complain about her boss to her family and others. Eventually, Darlene saw herself in a position of complete helplessness. She sank lower and lower until one day she had a breakthrough. Darlene began to write down everything her boss asked of her and how quickly she accomplished what she was given. She did this for a few weeks.

One day her boss called her into the office, and Darlene brought her log with her. Her boss berated her for her lack of work. When she was through, Darlene took out her log and read it to her boss. Her boss sat back, seemingly stunned that Darlene had everything written down. Her boss didn't apologize but never called her back into the office. When Darlene was through reading, she no longer felt like a victim. She'd taken the power from her boss. By doing so, she'd put herself in control of her emotions and her life.

"What is the hidden opportunity within this situation?" That is the question. What in this situation can you control and find opportunity in? That is how you keep labels from sticking to you. It's not easy to find the positive when bad things happen. It's not easy to find a lesson learned when you feel devastated. It doesn't matter if it's easy. What matters is that it can be done. It can and will be done by you. You have to believe that there is a lesson in everything that happens. You have to believe that everything that happens in your life will make you stronger.

When an accident occurs, the first person to arrive with some type of medical training is called a first responder. First responders can be police, firefighters, or trained civilians. They are there because they have had training to help the injured person until a more qualified professional arrives. They do not react to a situation; they respond.

One afternoon there is a loud crashing sound as a car hits a telephone pole. The man walking his dog around the neighborhood stops and stares. The woman waiting for the streetlight begins to scream. People on the sidewalks point and talk to each other. Other vehicles on the street stop. A man walks out of his store and becomes focused on the people in the vehicle. He doesn't scream but walks confidently toward the wreckage. This is the first responder. Let's take a look at the term *first responder* and what makes them different from the others on the street. First responders are people who have prepared, through taking classes and participating in drills, to treat victims of accidents before additional help comes to the scene.

The difference between first responders and the folks on the street is that first responders are prepared to deal with the emergency at hand. They are confident that they know what to do because they have studied and planned for it.

It's all about awareness and understanding that you control your life. One of the best ways to illustrate this is to fast for twenty-four hours by abstaining from food and drink. You choose whether to put food or drink into your body. No one else makes that choice. When the twenty-four hours is over, you know that you are in control. You chose to not eat the cake. You chose to not drink the orange juice. You were successful because of your choices. You also gained the health benefits of a twenty-four-hour fast. You are now stronger mentally and physically because of your success.

When you are in control and someone cuts you off in traffic, instead of getting angry by honking the horn and cursing, you respond by assuming the person's innocence. It might be that this person is racing to the emergency room to be with a loved one or is having a bad day and didn't see you. Either way, when you're in control, you respond instead of react.

Every small victory adds to your confidence. You will find that you are not only in control, but you are also building your foundation to believe you can do anything. And when you believe you can do anything, you always respond to a situation with confidence.

Chapter Seven

TAKING STEPS

The journey of a thousand miles begins with one step.

— Lao Tzu —

ACH JANUARY or New Year's Eve, people decide to make New Year's resolutions, and they start to make a list of the things they want to achieve in the next year. An article published in the *Journal of Clinical Psychology* provides some interesting statistics concerning Americans and New Year's resolutions. Forty-five percent of Americans usually make New Year's Resolutions and 17 percent make them infrequently, for a total of about 62 percent of Americans—but only 8 percent succeed with their resolutions. That's a pretty sobering thought. Think about the times you have made a resolution. Did you succeed? Are you one of the 8 percent who succeed, or one of the 54 percent who do not?

Making the resolution is the easy part. Keeping it is the hard part.

Napoleon Hill, author of *Think and Grow Rich*, once asked an audience, "What is the average number of times a person tries to achieve a new goal before they give up?" The audience guessed many times before he gave the answer: "Less than one."

It's all about taking the first step. I've learned in my life that 100 percent of the people who don't take the first step never take the second. It seems obvious, but many people become so focused on the result that they never take the first step, because it becomes too overwhelming even before they even have a chance to begin.

Think about babies learning to walk. They get up, they fall, they cry, they get back up. They fall again and get back up. They don't know fear of failure. They don't understand lack of success. They only know they want to walk. And eventually they do.

Don't be afraid to fall—everyone does. It's getting and taking the first step that's the most important. Take the step and then take another. Whether you fall in between doesn't matter. It's the fact that you take the step that counts.

Life Is the Longest Staircase

The longest staircase in the world, consisting of 11,674 steps, is located on Mount Niesen in the Swiss Alps. Every day of the year a funicular—two cable cars that counterbalance each other as one goes up and one goes down—takes people to the top of the mountain and back down. The staircase, on the other hand, is open to the public for a run just one day each year—one day. On this one day, people line up, raring to climb those 11,674 steps during the few hours it is open. For one day only, they can run to the top of the mountain rather than ride.

Just imagine yourself at the bottom of these stairs, wanting to get to the top. Could you do it without practicing and running stairs every day? Would it be possible if you hadn't trained? Could you just run those stairs, or would it require planning, training, and a desire?

Running to the top of Mount Niesen is no different than quitting smoking. Every goal has steps that have to be taken in order to achieve success.

Around the Block to a Marathon

When my wife, Andrea, started running, she'd never run more than a mile at a time in her entire life. She'd never thought of running a 5K, which is 3.1 miles or about 3,900 steps. She didn't believe that she could do it, but her trainer kept pushing her, and after training for it, she ran her first 5K. Following that, her trainer pushed her to run a few more steps each day, and in time she was ready to run a 10K (about 7,800 steps). From there she began to run longer training runs and was able to run for ten miles. With that goal accomplished, she signed up to run a half marathon—13.1 miles or about 16,500 steps—and she completed that. Thoroughly convinced she'd reached her peak performance, she continued to run for enjoyment and to stay in running shape.

I was training for a marathon at that time and had a long run of 18 miles planned. She decided to come along on the training run, with the understanding that she would walk when she couldn't run anymore. She pushed on and was able to run the entire 18 miles. It was at that point she finally believed she could run an entire marathon. Prior to that day she'd believed a marathon was impossible for her. With every mile she completed, every step she ran, her confidence grew. She ran her first of sixteen marathons after that. In the course of one year she went from starting to run to running a marathon. She went from believing she could not run 3 miles to running 26.2 miles, or about 33,000 steps.

It all began with taking one step after another. Taking the first step propelled her into taking another and another. With each step she gained confidence and belief in herself.

EXERCISE: Steps to the Mountaintop

You have to remember that you don't get to the top of the mountain without starting with a step. It doesn't matter where on the mountain you are at the moment, because you still have to take the first step and then the second. You get to the top by stepping.

Now it's time for you to take the first step. Remember that the first step leads to the second.

The steps to setting a goal are always the same:

1. List your goal in the present tense.

   _____

2. List the benefits of reaching your goal.

   _____

3. List the obstacles to achieving your goal.

   _____

Right now I want you to decide on one goal you have.

Write it down: _____

Now write it in the present tense as though you have already achieved it:

_____

Here's an example. Mary wants to lose 10 pounds. She now weighs 135 pounds.

Her goal is: *I weigh 125 pounds!*

It's time for you to get started. Write down your goal as though it has already happened.

Smile. Now that you have taken the first step, you are one step closer to achieving your goal than you were before.

Visualizing Steps

Guang Yue, PhD, is an exercise psychologist who studies cognitive motor function training. This is repetitive mental performance of forceful muscle contraction: visualization by another name. He has found that such visualization can strengthen muscles. In a study of normal people, he "compared people who went to the gym with people who carried out virtual workouts in their heads." The results were a 30 percent gain in muscle for those who went to the gym and a 13.5 percent gain in muscle in those who only visualized. The effects of the visualization lasted for three months. But notice that the visualization technique didn't last forever. Everyday hard work will sustain you, while visualization will help you. By combining them, you can achieve your goal.

These results are being studied in protocols to help the elderly and those who have experienced strokes, to see how visualization may help these populations live better lives.

Many studies have shown that doing both exercise and visualization is the most effective way to increase performance. That's why so many professional athletes use this powerful combination.

Brain studies have also been used to validate the use of visualization. The first step in visualization is from the old adage, "Seeing is believing." Visualization is one element to motivation, and while the use of visualization alone is not the answer, it is an element to achieving success.

The physiology of visualization shows that the neurons in the brain that transmit information perceive or "see" the imaged act exactly as they do the actual physical action. When you visualize an act, the neurons create a new neural pathway. This pathway consists of clusters of cells working together to create memories of a specific movement or behavior, so that when that actual situation occurs, your body reacts in the way the brain remembers.

In order to realize your goals, you must map out the steps to achieving them. It's the same with visualization. You read about visualizing the ultimate goal earlier in the chapter. Now I want you to visualize the incremental steps to achieving your ultimate goal. Visualize each step in a positive way. By doing this you will maintain your motivation and more greatly ensure overall success.

Remember, there are no shortcuts to success. The Law of the Harvest always applies. Visualization is one component in achieving your dreams. There is no substitute for working hard, training, and mastering skills. By using all the tools you have learned, you have increased your power to succeed.

Visualization can work for everyone. It works in business, it works in sports, and it is even used in the medical community.

The Miracle Man

In the 1970s Morris E. Goodman began a sales career in insurance. Within a year he made the Million Dollar Round Table. In 1981 he purchased his own airplane and became a pilot. On a leisurely flight, his plane experienced engine troubles and lost power. Goodman tried to make an emergency landing, but the plane crashed. He lived through the crash, but he was completely paralyzed—unable to move from head to foot, unable even to breathe, talk, or swallow on his own. The only thing he could do was blink his eyes.

After he was found and was placed in medical care, his sister realized Goodman was trying to communicate through blinking, so she created a series of charts with letters and subjects, each with a corresponding number. Goodman was able to communicate by blinking his eyes in correlation with the charts.

As he improved, Goodman was transferred to another hospital. He realized in order to speak he had to be able to breathe on his own, so he found a way to use muscles other than his diaphragm to breathe. After weeks of practice and visualization, he was able to take his first breath. The doctors were shocked and in time began to wean him off the ventilator. His first word was "Mama."

From the hospital he was sent to a rehabilitation center. There he began to visualize himself walking. Even though his doctors insisted his left side would be permanently paralyzed, he proved them wrong by walking out of the hospital unassisted by the end of the year.

Through visualization and hard work, Morris Goodman proved the doctors wrong. He did the impossible and along the way earned the nickname of "The Miracle Man."

Skills

Are you born with the ability to do something? What are the skills you develop through practice? Are you born being nice, or is it learned? Is being good at math something you are born with, or is it a skill that is practiced and developed?

First let's define skill. According to Webster's dictionary, a skill is "a learned power of doing something competently; a developed aptitude or ability."

And aptitude is defined as "capacity for learning." Everyone has aptitude. Because everyone has aptitude, everyone has the ability to learn and perfect skills. Not everyone will do it at the same pace or in the same way, but everyone can do it.

It's said that Mozart played the piano when he was young, but he didn't have any compositions in print until about ten years later. When he was young, his father helped him to learn and encouraged his son's passion. Mozart practiced for hours every day, and it took ten years before he wrote his first piece of music unassisted. A certain percentage of people—for example, some of those with autism—are born with a specific skill or aptitude. It could be that they can play the piano the first time they try. So certainly some people are born with a very specific skill. What is interesting about this "savant syndrome" is that the skill displayed, although very deep, is extremely narrow. This basically means that they have one very specific skill but no others. Internationally acclaimed psychologist Michael Howe said in New Scientist magazine, "The main difference between experts and savants is that savants do things which most of us couldn't be bothered to get good at."

Your life has a purpose and you clarify that purpose. You choose what you want, and you work to get it. By being aware of what you want, you clarify the outline of your life. When you have an outline of your life, you fill in the areas to get to where you want to go. You have to know where you're going so you can master the skills you need to get there.

If you were going on vacation, you would plan when and where you want to go. From there you would decide how to get there, how long to stay, where to stay—and all of this would be based on how much money you had to spend. It's the same in achieving your goals in life. In order to get to where you're going, you must be able to pay your way. That means you need to have the skills required to get to where you want to go.

You can learn skills. Remember that. You can have anything you want; you just have to work for it. It doesn't matter where you start, whether you have a natural ability or not—none of that matters in the end. The only thing that does matter is the amount of work you put in. You have the ability; now you need to work.

Some of you might be saying, "Well, I just want money. How's that a skill?" Wanting money requires that you master many skills in order to achieve the goal of having money.

As you study individuals who are wealthy or have money, you'll understand that they have skills that you'll need to learn. You'll need to develop the skill of a good work ethic, to put in the required time. You'll have to develop the skill of communicating with others. People will need to like you. You'll need to learn the skill of dedication. It will take all of these skills and more. As you study, you'll discover individuals who have what you want, and you need to follow the things they've done. All the things they've done are skills you will need to learn.

Some people are going to learn much more quickly than you. But again, it's a talent that's overrated. Someone may have some kind of talent or may be better than you initially. If you continue to put in the time and the effort, eventually you'll surpass them. Remember that skill is learned. Someone else may start out at a higher level, but if you start out knowing that you can learn the skill, you have the advantage. You know you can do it. You know you can surpass them.

I get sick and tired of hearing people say, "He's just got so much natural ability; if only we could get him to apply himself." Give me the kid who'll put the time in. Give me the kid who will put the work into it. You can help sculpt that kid into being the best, but for the person who has initial talent, the likelihood is that everything in life came easily to him so he never learned how to work. Initial talent will carry you only so far. I don't know anybody at the top of his field to whom it just miraculously one day "happened." He was passionate about something and put the time and effort into it. Most important, he worked at it over and over and over again.

It's a skill, my friend. It's a skill and you can learn it and master it.

10,000 Is Just a Number

Whatever skill set you want—whether it's being happy, being healthy, being wealthy, being debt free, making a difference in people's lives—it is something you can learn to do.

Malcolm Gladwell writes about the 10,000 Hour Rule in his book *Outliers*. The theory is, to become the very, very best at something or become someone in the top percent, you have to practice that something for at least 10,000 hours to get there. If you don't really like something, it's likely that you are not going to spend time doing it. It isn't that you're not good at it, it's that you don't like to do it and therefore you probably won't put any time into it. If you are passionate about something, then putting in the time is easy. Every hour you take to excel comes effortlessly.

When you think of the 10,000 hours needed to hone a skill, it may seem overwhelming. But if you think of those 10,000 hours in terms of a staircase, you can visualize it. Every step you climb is one step closer to the top. Two thousand steps into the climb, you can see things from a different angle. You can look and see how far you've come and how far you still need to go.

Ten thousand is just a number. Every step forward is one less step to take. Nine thousand nine hundred ninety-nine is a number, the same as nine thousand nine hundred ninety-eight. They are numbers that you can and will achieve; all you have to do is take the first step and start counting.

The "Talent" Trick

Usually people who choose to go to beauty school have already put in hundreds of hours of practice before they enroll in school. Many of those attending school have been doing hair, makeup, and nails since they were young. So when they get to beauty school they have a certain number of hours already under their belt. Others look at them and say, "They have a knack for it." The truth is, they really liked it, so they spent hours doing it. Their passion drove them to find time to do it. It's no wonder they are pretty good at it before they get to beauty school. Once they get there, they learn the fundamentals and they clock in to get their required hours of training. While doing this they are continuing to add hours outside school.

By the time they graduate, when you factor in the time they spent as a child, the time in school, and the time spent outside school, they potentially have put in over 4,000 hours. This is not to say that when they graduate they are going to be Vidal Sassoon, as he had a lifetime of study. They're not going to be Paul Mitchell. These two put years and years into their craft to become the very best at what they do. What it does mean is that the beauty school graduate is on her way to achieving the 10,000 hours.

Remember what I said at the beginning. Skill is learned. You can learn it. You will learn whatever skill you want.

The "Special" in "Special Ed Kid"

From the University of Michigan comes this story in the words of the girl who lived it. "After checking that the Scotch tape had sufficiently secured the paper to the refrigerator, I stepped back to admire my accomplishments. I scanned the perfectly aligned report cards and essay grades and felt a satisfying sense of achievement. I could feel my sister's eyes glaring at me from a few feet away. I know she thinks I'm bragging by plastering the refrigerator with my academic achievements, but to me, they mean so much more than a job well done. The wall of paper serves as a constant reminder of how far I have grown since I was classified as a Special Education student.

"It was only first grade; how different could I be from everyone else? Everything seemed fine to me, until I was brought to a meeting with my teacher and my parents for an unexpected agenda. At the meeting, they told me that I was going to repeat the first grade. Expecting tears, my teacher and my parents were shocked to see my eyes light up with the thought of watching baby chicks hatch one more time. At first, I even considered myself lucky to be the only one of my friends who was able to experience playing the role of both a Native American and a Pilgrim at Thanksgiving dinner. My perception of myself as lucky changed for me in the third grade when, as I read to my kindergarten partner during story time, she became impatient with my inarticulate reading and began to correct my speech. It was then that I knew I was different.

"As I continued to find school frustrating, my teachers' concerns grew and ultimately resulted in an education evaluation. While other students my age view such an experience negatively, I felt fortunate that someone was finally going to validate and explain my learning issues. My challenges were confirmed as the testing revealed a learning disability that had caused my below-average skills.

"Unlike many of my peers in Special Education, I grew to accept my weaknesses at an early age. While many of my friends spent their summers at sleep-away camps, I was enrolled in a reading camp and took on extra schoolwork during my summers. While others were reluctant to enter the resource room, fearing embarrassment, I was eager to embrace the support and utilize the skills that would unlock a world of knowledge. I began to feel proud of my success in the special education program, and used that feeling of accomplishment to push myself even further. Employing all the strategies I had learned over the years, I focused on compensating for my weaknesses by capitalizing on my strengths. As a result of my success in the special education program, I was declassified in the eighth grade. While I had some fears about entering high school without extra support, I knew the work ethic I had developed would continue to grow and get stronger as I became more confident in my abilities. After overcoming my greatest challenge, I now know that I can accomplish any task, no matter how great. The proof? It's right there on the refrigerator."

The whole secret to success is that you can become whoever you want to become. You can accomplish whatever you want to accomplish by understanding that it is a skill, and that means it can be learned. Think about the preceding story. A child took the journey of learning many new skills. A child, classified as learning disabled, achieved success. This helps prove that there is nothing in this world you cannot do, nothing you cannot achieve, as long as you work at it. Everything is possible for you. *Everything*—if you will work for it.

Dollars Follow Value

One of the universal principles in life is "Dollars follow value." As you work on your skill set, you will find that you're becoming more valuable to the world, to the people in your family, to your friends, to your coworkers, to your employer and employees, to your stockholders, and so on. As you grow more capable of creating value for other people, the more valuable you become yourself. The more valuable you become, the more dollars will come to you.

Do you really think you're just going to get a job if you're not working? If it were me, and I were out of a job, I'd go to work somewhere for free and try to create so much value that they would have to pay me. It's something I've done before.

I wanted to be a waiter at Pizza Hut because I wanted to work for tips. I knew that I would be the best waiter they'd ever had, so I knew I could make good money waiting tables. The problem was, Pizza Hut wasn't hiring. I went in every single day and asked, "When are you going to hire me?" Every day I got the same answer, "We're not hiring." That didn't dissuade me at all. One day I went in and the manager said she had a filthy, disgusting drain full of hair, grease, oil, and food that needed to be cleaned and if I cleaned it she would give me ten dollars. Without hesitation I said, "Let's do it." So I went into the back, put on gloves, got out the Clorox, and cleaned that drain until it was completely unclogged and clean. When I was done cleaning she said that she hadn't really expected me to do it. She offered me the ten dollars and I turned it down. I told her that I wanted to be a waiter. She told me she didn't need a waiter, but she did need a cook. I told her I'd take the position, but that my goal was to be a waiter for her.

I wasn't on the schedule very often and I wanted more hours. I put a note on the employee calendar that said if anyone wanted to take the weekends off, I would work for them. Most everyone wanted the weekends off, so I was able to work more hours than I'd been scheduled for originally. One Friday night, a waitress didn't show up for work and they couldn't get anyone to cover. I was there as a cook and asked if I could wait the tables instead. The manager told me she needed someone to cook, so I took the initiative to have another cook cover for me and I waited the tables.

I was the best waiter they'd ever had that night. I kept the tables clean, people didn't have to wait for their drinks, I brought their food quickly and checked back often to be certain they had everything they wanted. After that night, I wasn't put on the schedule as a waiter, only as a cook. But the door was already open. I put notes on the employee calendar offering to work waiter shifts, especially on weekends, for anyone who wanted the time off. Eventually I was hired as a waiter and it was all because I started with cleaning a disgusting drain.

When Kristi Mailioux first joined Molly Maids twenty years ago as a receptionist, she made a choice to be a great employee. She was only going to be a temporary employee; she was planning on going back to college to get her master's degree in social work. She stayed only because the owner of Molly Maids offered to pay her tuition if she stayed one year. During that year, she worked not only as the receptionist, but also doing other chores assigned to her, including making coffee, greeting guests, entering data, and cleaning toilets. In an interview with *Business News Daily*, Mailioux said, "No task should ever be beneath you. When I began at Molly Maids, I was the receptionist and I had to clean the bathrooms." Today, Kristi Mailioux is the president of Molly Maids and oversees the operations of the entire maid service franchise.

You have to start somewhere. It doesn't matter where the starting line is; just get started and good things will come. Remember, it's one step after another. You have to take step one to get to step two.

LeBron James Knows Value

Why does NBA superstar LeBron James make so much money? It's because he creates value for all the spectators who want to watch him and who get excited about his greatness. With his skills, he's creating a ton of value, which in turn brings in dollars. He creates so much value that it reaches a whole new level. He has Fortune 500 companies paying him millions of dollars in endorsements each year because of the influence and the value he brings to the company. If he is drinking Powerade, then other people want to drink Powerade. Dollars follow value.

Bleacherreports.com's article "Doing the Math on What LeBron James Would Be Worth on the Open Market" states, "LeBron James is the most underpaid player in the NBA. . . . He simply brings that much value." Forbes says that LeBron is the world's fourth-highest-paid athlete. Now, saying that he's being underpaid as the world's fourth highest paid athlete is a big statement.

What exactly gives LeBron this distinction? There are several reasons, beginning with endorsements. When LeBron graduated from high school, Nike gave him a seven-year, ninety-million-dollar deal that turned out to be one of the best bargains the company ever made, given the revenue increases they've reported ever since. He also endorses Sprite, McDonald's, Powerade, and Bubblicious, giving them incredible value by increasing their revenue. Underpaid at ninety million dollars—wow.

Another reason he is so valuable is that he brings fans to watch him play. When LeBron played for the Cleveland Cavaliers, the year he left they were second in attendance in the NBA. Today, without him, they rank nineteenth. Since he went to Miami, the Miami Heat attendance numbers have increased, bringing more ticket sales, increased revenue, and value to the franchise.

The amount of NBA merchandise his name sells also increases his value. There are jerseys, bobbleheads, T-shirts, and so on, each item again bringing in revenue and value.

The NBA television contract is now $930 million a year, and in 2016 when it expires, *Forbes* has predicted the broadcast rights will sell for $1.2 billion. Since LeBron has joined the NBA, its popularity keeps increasing. According to Bleacherreports.com, "it might be the figure that best shows how much value LeBron has; by 2016, he may add almost $1 million per year in revenue to the teams he doesn't even play for." Again, he's increasing revenue for the entire NBA and all the teams.

LeBron didn't just "luck" his way into this position. He put in over 10,000 hours before he even entered the NBA, and he still works on his game. When his team, the Miami Heat, lost to the Dallas Mavericks in the 2011 NBA finals, he didn't say, "We'll get them next year." Instead he went to Hakeem Olajuwon, arguably one of the best centers to ever play in the NBA and a 2008 inductee into the Basketball Hall of Fame, and asked for help in improving his post game so he could get better and better.

For me, that's what makes LeBron James great. He didn't stop learning. He saw that he needed to improve on another skill set and worked on it. In the midst of the pain and agony of losing his second NBA final, rather than wallowing in pity or accepting that he was a finalist, he strove to better his game and found an expert to help him.

As you read in the opening story, you can have everything you want. You just have to put in the time, the effort, and the sacrifice. Your refrigerator door is waiting for your report card.

Things Will Get Easier

Great guitar playing doesn't just happen overnight. It takes hours and hours of practice. But in those first few weeks, there is a problem that every novice guitarist faces: sensitive fingertips. Because the fingertips are the way the musician "frets" the note, the fingertips have to become tougher. Those first few days are not a pleasant experience. There is a fine line between the beginning of calluses and bleeding blisters.

Building calluses comes down to consistent playing, day after day. It takes perseverance and determination to build the calluses required to play for longer periods of time. That means playing until the fingertips hurt and then coming back the next day.

Once calluses are formed, the guitarist can play for longer times and take on more challenging music. The really great thing about getting calluses is that guitarists are achieving more than just forming calluses; they are also getting practice.

Calluses don't happen just with musicians. They happen, metaphorically, with everything you routinely do. As you repeat your actions over and over, habits take root. Things that were once painful are no longer so because you are tougher and more experienced.

When my daughter Whitney was seven years old, we bought the Wii from Nintendo. Remembering how fun Mike Tyson's Punch-Out was for me as a kid, I had to buy the game for my kids. At the very beginning she could not even defeat the first opponent and was saying how hard it was, how she couldn't do it; I told her it would take practice and that she would need to learn the skills in order to defeat the fighters. She would need to put the required time and practice over and over and over again to increase her ability to beat the fighters in the game. It didn't take her long before she developed those skills and achieved her goal of beating all the fighters in the game.

For the abilities you want to master, look to build calluses in your life by making those activities a habit. The act of building calluses will allow you to spend more time doing what you love, and once you have those calluses you'll know you're on your way to mastery.

Celebrating Small Victories

Everything you have or do in life is because of you. Whatever you believe is what you're going to get. When you believe you can have it all, you will have it all, as long as you're also remembering the last part, that you just have to work for it.

One of the interesting things I've seen in people who don't believe is that their actions keep this lack of belief alive. When you don't believe, you don't work for anything, and you get exactly what you believe. So by not believing, you have a built-in excuse not to work, and it becomes a cycle. Don't believe, don't work, don't achieve, don't believe.

Now, on the flip side, when you believe, it is still a cycle. You believe, you work, you succeed, you believe. Every single time you succeed in your life, your belief becomes stronger. That is why it is so important to take note of your small victories. You don't need to have a parade, but you do need to acknowledge the fact that you've succeeded and continue the steps to your goal. With this positive attitude, you will work harder and therefore achieve your goals faster, and your belief will become stronger. The stronger your belief, the bigger your goals, the more you achieve, and again your belief grows.

Your life is not complete. You have much to do, much to achieve, much to build. Think of your life in terms of a construction site. Your goal is the building. Your affirmations are the hard hat you wear on the site. The work you put in constructs the building, and your belief is the ground it's built on. You don't enter a construction site without a hard hat, so keep those affirmations at the ready whenever you enter into a situation where you're striving to build or achieve something, especially a situation that might intimidate you or contain obstacles. Keep constructing your life, using all the tools you have.

EXERCISE: Have a Party!

It's important to celebrate victories along the way. Something as small as drinking a glass of water when your goal is to become healthier deserves a pat on the back.

With every forward step you take, you are closer to your goal. Every single step is a win, so take the time and celebrate your wins while still moving forward.

There are many ways to celebrate:

- Call a friend and tell him why you are celebrating.
- Have a goal wall and with every goal achieved put a sticky note on the wall.
- Take an hour to do something for yourself.
- Look in the mirror and tell yourself how amazing you are!

Chapter Eight

TIME MANAGEMENT

We first make our habits, then our habits make us.

— JOHN DRYDEN —

CONTROLLING YOUR TIME is one of the most important things you can do. You can read books and listen to tapes to help you learn the skill of time management. Several different types of planners can help you better control your time: day planners, monthly planners, and apps that help you with scheduling. Regardless of what type of planner you choose, just using it will help you use your time more efficiently. This is because you are now aware of your time.

You also need to understand that controlling your time is not the same thing as scheduling your time. Controlling your time means you know what items are priority items, and you schedule them accordingly. I write the six most important things I need to get done the following day the night before. Doing this allows my subconscious mind to start working on those things while I sleep. The night before, you can also put out the items you will need first thing in the morning when you get to work. That way there is no wasted time or energy looking for what you need to complete your task.

Every single person on this earth could schedule twenty-four hours of his or her day every day of the year. Does that mean they are being productive or controlling time? No! It simply means they are accounting for what they do or scheduling their time. In order to control time, you have to know what you want to achieve, how long it will take to achieve it, and how it fits into your overall strategy. You need to know what items take priority over others. You need to understand that controlling your time includes scheduling, but that it's more than just scheduling the time.

Habits

When you think about how you live each day, you will see that your habits establish how you use your time for most of your day. If you get up and habitually brush your teeth before eating breakfast, that is your habit. One day, if you don't brush your teeth when you first get up, something seems amiss in your life.

If your habits are constructive, meaning they help you achieve the goals you have in life, they are good for you. If they stop your progress toward your goals, then you need to change them. You have the ultimate power to change your habits, and in changing your habits, you have the power to change your life.

About three years ago, I decided to stop watching television. I love watching television, because it allows me to turn my brain off, watch sporting events, and relax. But as much as I enjoy it, I love spending time with my family more. No one asked me to stop watching TV; I didn't have to stop, but I knew that in order to spend more time with my family, something I value much higher than TV, I needed to make a change. Now if I'm watching TV, I'm watching movies with my family and on occasion watching a prerecorded sporting event. I haven't seen the Super Bowl live in three years.

As you can see, I'm an all-or-nothing type of guy.

To give another personal example, I hate getting up in the morning and going to the gym. I would much rather spend my time in bed on my soft pillow, yet every day I am at the gym working out before many people are even out of bed. I do that because I put more value on the benefits of working out than on sleeping late in the morning. Working out gets my blood moving and makes me feel alive. After ten or twenty minutes I start feeling really good. The sense of accomplishment in completing my workout in addition to all the endorphins I get makes it worthwhile to me. I love the fact that I'm burning calories, that I'm working out, and that it is early in the day, even though I don't necessarily like waking up early.

All of this comes down to replacing a bad habit with a good one. We become a slave to our habits, whether they are good or bad. For example, when my family travels on vacation, we plan the time to go to the gym and work out. It's part of our trip and we schedule the time because it's a habit. We don't feel complete if we don't do it. We own it, because it's a facet of who we are, not something outside us.

If you want to quit smoking, then replace the bad habit of smoking with a new good habit like running or another form of exercise. Find that good habit that will increase your value to yourself and others. The key to replacing a habit is understanding why you want or need to replace it. The "why" is the motivation you will need. Once you break down the "why," you can focus on providing an answer in the form of a good habit.

For example, John is trying to stop drinking caffeine. The first thing he does every morning is make a fresh pot of coffee. Then he pours himself a cup, thinks about the day ahead of him, makes some plans for accomplishing his goals, takes a shower, and gets ready for work. When John thinks about his morning coffee, he associates it with the quiet time he uses to plan his day. Then he wonders, is the habit the coffee or is it the quiet time in the morning? The next day, he doesn't make a pot of coffee, and instead he pours himself a glass of water and sits down in his normal spot and has his quiet time. He notices that this doesn't have the same feel for him. The following morning he makes himself a cup of decaffeinated coffee and drinks it while having his quiet time to plan his day. That works for him. He has replaced his caffeine habit with a better habit.

Once habits are aligned with your goals, then they become productive and positive.

To be more specific, if your goal is to lose weight, your goal-aligned habits might include drinking eight glasses of water a day, tracking everything that you eat, and creating a habit of movement, whether it's just walking every day or going to the gym four or five days a week.

When you can create habits that align with your goals, success is inevitable. It's almost as if it's already accomplished.

If you are not there yet, remember: habits can be changed. Habits should be changed when they are not positive in your life, and you have the power to change them. You have the power to change your life. *Believe It* and take action.

A Catalyst for Change

Charles Duhigg, in his book *The Power of Habits*, uses the term *keystone habit*. This is a habit that creates a platform for other good habits. A keystone is the final wedge-shaped piece of a masonry arch that allows the arch to bear its own weight—both sides of the arch push against the keystone, which makes the entire arch stable. The word *keystone* is commonly used to describe the central supporting argument for any company or theory, because without the keystone, an arch or organization or theory would fail.

Think about your life and determine your keystone habits. Some examples of keystone habits are waking up at five in the morning; running four miles every Monday, Wednesday, and Friday; or meditating every day at noon. These habits are the platform for other habits. If you choose to wake up every morning at five and exercise from five thirty to seven, then you start your day already having completed your exercise goal.

The secret about keystone habits is that if you remove a keystone habit, everything surrounding that habit falls. This applies to both good and bad habits. If you are a smoker and decide to quit, thus removing the keystone of smoking, then other habits such as leaving meetings for smoke breaks, overloading on breath mints, and standing back from others all fall because you no longer smoke.

On the other hand, if your keystone habit is exercise and you stop, other habits change. You might now watch more television, eat the same amount of food and gain weight, decrease your stamina, or potentially change your sleep patterns. All this occurs because you no longer exercise.

When looking at change, you have to be aware of your keystone habits and how they contribute, positively or negatively, to the changes you make.

Change is about setting goals. You've learned that in order to achieve a goal you must define the goal, research how to accomplish the goal, and then take the first step, the second step, never stopping, always stepping. Remember the staircase—it's not how quickly you get to the top, it's the fact that you make it to the top.

Change is easiest when you align the change to a habit. You used this technique when you read your affirmations while you brushed your teeth. The habit was brushing, and the addition was reading or mentally saying your affirmation. Think about a change you need to make. Which habits could you align the change with?

Each change you make in your life will ignite another. If the changes you start with are positive, the following changes will be positive, too. It's like a string of firecrackers. When you light one, it lights another and another and so on. Live your life knowing you have the power to change whatever you want. Just have the courage to light the first firecracker.

Drug Dealing to Diploma

John was thirteen the first time he sold drugs to his older brother's friend. He wanted to be the "cool guy" who was popular. Through drug dealing he found popularity with some, but lost most of his childhood friends. He was the perfect mule for the dealers, being too young to get any prison time. Plus he would never snitch because he thought the dealers had his back. By the time he was fourteen, he was well known to law enforcement throughout the city.

John was sent to juvenile detention numerous times, each time receiving more accolades from his street friends. It wasn't a matter of if, but when he would go to jail. His parents had no idea how to get John to stop his behavior, and at fifteen he was sent to a treatment facility and eventually to a foster home.

His time in foster care was rocky. For the first two years he fought all attempts for help. Then one day he met a young woman who changed his life. She was his age and lived with her parents. She didn't do drugs or smoke and for whatever reason, she was attracted to John and they began to date.

At first, John had no idea how long they would be together. The days turned into weeks and they kept dating. John had never had a relationship last this long. He chose to never smoke around her or her family because he thought it was disrespectful, and in time he decided to stop completely. When he was able to kick that habit, he was surprised. It hadn't been his original intent, but now he was smoke free. He then began to think about what other aspects of his life he could change. He wanted his girlfriend to be proud of him. Then not only did he want his girlfriend to be proud, he also wanted his family to be proud. Before he'd been so ashamed of the things he had done, and it had been easier to just run away. But now, with his girlfriend by his side, he had hope that his life could change for the better.

John started to contemplate how his actions had gotten him into foster care and away from a family who loved him. It didn't happen overnight, but he made the first step to change his habits by deciding to stop selling drugs. John continued to make a conscious choice every day following that not to do or sell drugs. To make money, he got a job washing dishes at a local restaurant. The work was hard, and he made less in a week than he had made in a day while dealing. But it was honest work. For the first time in years, John was proud of how he made his money.

He went to school regularly and actually participated. He was able to leave foster care and reunite with his family for his senior year of high school. Now, through hard work, he is on track to graduate with his class. He still dates his girlfriend and they look forward to a bright future together. He plans to go to college and intends to pay his own way. In the future he would like to work with kids who made the same mistakes he did. When asked about his experience, he said, "I didn't make the right choices growing up. I hope that maybe someday I can help some kid change his life around before it's too late."

EXERCISE: The "Whys" of Your Habits

Take a look at what you want to change. Be very clear about what you want to change. Write it down.

_____

_____

_____

Now list at least two reasons why it's important to change.

_____

_____

_____

Now list how you are going to change the habit.

_____

_____

_____

Example 1: Nick wanted to quit smoking.

Why: It was unhealthy for him and others.

Why: He smelled like smoke all the time.

Nick chose to start using e-cigarettes, and he cut down on his nicotine according to the prescribed schedule. Now he has replaced smoking nicotine with just using e-cigarettes, his health is improved, and he doesn't smell like smoke all the time.

Example 2: Chris stays up and watches TV late at night. He finds he is tired every morning when he gets up for work and never seems to get his daily exercise in. He wants to be less tired and have more energy to work out.

Why: Too much late-night TV; not enough sleep

Why: No exercise; less healthy life

Chris chose to get up at five in the morning. The first morning it was hell. He'd gone to bed at 1:00 a.m. and was without sleep. By 6:30 a.m. he had completed his exercise for the day. That night at 9:00 p.m. he was screaming for the pillow and a good night's sleep. The next morning he forced himself to get up at five again and go to the gym. The keystone habit changed from negative to positive, as it changed both his sleeping habits and his daytime routine.

Prioritizing

There are so many things in life that come at you. It is your choice to take what you want and leave the rest behind. There are steps that lead you forward, and distractions coming from all directions that can take you off the path.

Have you ever noticed how you always see teenagers with a phone or music earbuds in their ears? I know a teenager who chose not to interact on Facebook, Twitter, Tumblr, Pinterest, or any other social media. She even turns off her cell phone at night and puts it in another room to charge. I asked her why she does this. "It's pretty simple. If I had to keep track of all the things going on around me, I'd never get the important things done. That's just too much for me to think about."

It wasn't something I'd expected to hear. So I asked her, "Isn't it hard to do that?"

"Yeah, I guess," she replied. "But I just don't have time for all that stuff. I have things I want to accomplish. I hear things all the time; I'm just not the first one to hear it, and I'm good with that. By the time it gets to me, it's usually all over. It's a lot less pressure."

I thought about her choices. She didn't use the word *distraction* or *drift*. She just said it was too much. And being too much meant it stopped her from doing what she wanted. There are all kinds of words and names for things that keep you from staying on track toward your goals. Whatever the words are, it all comes down to this: it's too much stuff.

One of my favorite sayings is, "If you want to get something done, give it to the busiest person." That is true! Busy people learn to use their time efficiently in order to accomplish more than most people. Busy people have purpose. They have a reason to be busy, to have a schedule. That's why they can accomplish so much and even more when needed. They know how to prioritize and how to be flexible. They are not afraid to move out of their comfort zone when it's required. The amazing thing about the busiest person is that she has exactly the same twenty-four hours in a day that you have.

Prioritizing and flexibility are both skills you can learn. People aren't just born with these skills. They are honed through hard work and time. Use the experiences of others to help you master these skills. Watch successful people and figure out how they accomplish so much in the same twenty-four hours as everyone else. No one gets extra time for good behavior. Determine how time contributes to the choices you make in life. Then make a plan to use your time wisely and *do it*.

A Day Is Always 24 Hours

Here's the truth about time. Unless you write it down and track it, you will have no idea where your time goes. There is no way to keep track of time by simply trying to remember what happened. It is impossible. That is why you should use a time log or some way to track your precious time in writing. I guarantee that the first time you do this, you will be shocked about how you spend your time.

A normal scenario can go like this: You go to the grocery store to pick up one item. You allocate ten minutes in the store. Once there, you start moving up and down the aisles, and you start shopping for things other than what you came in for. When you get to the checkout line, with twenty items instead of one, you still think you're doing okay on time. Then you meet a friend and spend ten minutes catching up. By the time you get back to the car with your bags of groceries and look at the clock, thirty minutes is gone. How do you make up those twenty minutes? If you weren't taking stock of what time you went in the store and what time you came out, you would remember it as simply ten minutes, the time you had originally planned.

There's an interesting principle called the *Pareto principle*. Vilfredo Pareto was a nineteenth-century scholar who discovered that the things that are critical to any set of elements are usually in the minority. As people looked at this principle, it evolved into the 80/20 rule. Eighty percent of the value comes from 20 percent of the items, while the other 20 percent of the value comes from 80 percent of the items. This is true whether you're talking about pea pods or sales in a store—with peapods, about 80 percent of peas come from 20 percent of the pods, and in a store, about 80 percent of sales come from 20 percent of the customers. In other words, 80 percent of your output comes from 20 percent of your effort.

Just how does this apply to me, you wonder? It's simple. Look at how you spend your time most of the day, the 80 percent. Then look at what you accomplished in that time. Now look at the 20 percent of the day, where you invested your time. Odds are that 80 percent of what you accomplished came about because of the 20 percent of time you wisely invested. You need to look at the 80 percent of the time you don't use as wisely and make adjustments to invest yourself.

Steven Covey made this point by saying, "The main thing is to keep the main thing the main thing."

EXERCISE: Track Your Time

The night before, write down the six most important things you have to do tomorrow. You always have a do-it-now list, but the night before, choose the six most important things to do the next day. Do them right away, and cross them off the list.

Always remember, first things first. Accomplish the things you need to do, and then whatever little pebbles fall in are okay.

Using a time management system will help you. It can be an app or a written log. If you can't seem to figure out where your time is going, I suggest you try this. The night before, write down your top six things you have to do in the morning. Put them in your log with an estimation of the time they will take. When they are completed, then log what you do for the remainder of the day. Within a week you'll see exactly where your time is going.

From that point on you will always do your top six things from the night before, then move on to your do-it-now list. This will keep you moving in a positive direction. You will find that by doing this, you will be able to do more things and when that something extra comes up, you will have the time to do it.

Procrastination

Procrastination is like ignoring a dragon. When the dragon first comes out of its egg, it's cute, like all babies are cute. It might blow some smoke and a bit of flame but nothing too dramatic. Because the dragon is still small, there's no hurry. Within a week, the dragon can hiss more fire, but still, with a bit of skill you can stay away. By the end of the first month, the dragon is big, the flames shooting from his mouth hurt like hell, and you have a big problem on your hands. If only you'd taken care to slay him when he was small and easily managed. Procrastination in slaying a dragon can cause serious injury, both mentally and physically.

We all have our dragons. In fact, most of us have more than one. It's how you deal with them when they first show up that determines whether they grow and become dangerous. Get the things that make you uncomfortable tamed at the beginning. When you don't allow procrastination, the dragons in your life will not grow.

It's amazing how important little things become when you're facing a big problem or decision. Suddenly, you focus on a task that never was that important in the first place. All the little tasks are easily done and put out of the way, while the big task you are trying to escape never leaves, it just keeps getting bigger, at least in your mind. Slay that dragon right now. The bigger he grows, the harder he will be to manage.

Choosing to slay your dragons early is a habit, and it can be done. First you have to admit to yourself that they exist. Once you do that, you can find a way to get those unpleasant tasks completed. In my case, I choose to do the toughest thing first. This wasn't my first instinct; I had to choose it. If the task is too big to swallow in one gulp, break it into manageable pieces. Everything in life is composed of parts of various sizes.

Slay Your Dragons

I always plan on doing the most uncomfortable task first thing in the morning. Brian Tracy calls this "swallowing the frog." The idea being, if you are uncomfortable with doing something, you tend to avoid it. If you put it off all day, you spend your day thinking about it. The anticipation of doing it creates stress and anxiety. The greatest gift you can give yourself in this situation it to just do it first thing. It's crossed off your list and you can go on to accomplish what you need without added stress.

It's kind of like having an appointment for a root canal. It's not something I look forward to, so I set my appointment for the first thing in the morning. That way, it's over and done with before my day is even halfway done. I can move on to what I need to accomplish without the imagined sound of the dentist's drill ringing in my head.

Make Yourself Uncomfortable

Being uncomfortable is one of the greatest gifts the universe will offer you. When you're uncomfortable it means it's time for you to grow. Let's put this in the context of a typical day. The first things people tend to do are the things that are easy, and those things usually can wait. They tend to put off the "high priority" items, things that have to be done because they are hard or just outside the comfort zone. Don't procrastinate with these items. They are only going to get bigger and bigger in your imagination.

For example, Kevin is the number one real estate agent in Utah and has gone through a coaching program for real estate agents. This is a gentleman who makes seven figures and does very well. I asked him what he does that other real estate agents don't do. He answered, "Cold calls." He went on to say that most real estate agents are not willing to call homeowners who are selling their home themselves, without an agent. But he is willing to do this, and he makes a hundred cold calls every day four days per week. No one else wants to make the calls, but a top-selling successful real estate agent is willing to. Through practice he's become very good at it, even though it made him uncomfortable when he started. He said his success is because he will do what others won't because they are uncomfortable.

EXERCISE: Bite-Size Your Life

If you look at what is making you uncomfortable and break it into smaller pieces, it's not such a big problem anymore. You can even think of tackling your problems like eating a steak. If you put the whole steak in your mouth, you will choke, and in the end, you will hate the steak. If you cut it into smaller manageable bites, you can savor each piece for as long as you want. When you have finished, it's been a much more pleasurable experience. As with anything in life, you have to get started and you have to keep going until it's done. However you have to break it down, you can do it. I know you can. It has been done before and you can do it now. In order to bite-size your life, you need to look at the goal and begin to break it down.

Example 1: Ashley wants to save money. The prospect is overwhelming to her, because she never has money and always seems to be floating in her checking account, praying that the last check has not cleared yet. She goes to a payday loan company to get advances on her paycheck. The idea of being able to ever save money continues to feel impossible. Ashley could break her goal into the following steps:

Step 1: Keep track of spending using a log of every place she spends money—restaurants, gas, dry cleaner, movies, everything.

Step 2: Look at each expense and be aware of where her money is going.

Step 3: Determine what is important and what is not.

Step 4: Take the money not spent and put it in a savings account.

Example 2: Paul wants to lose weight. He procrastinates because it's easier to sit. Paul could break his goal into the following steps:

Step 1. Keep bottled water with him at all times.

Step 2: Keep raw almonds around to curb his hunger.

Step 3: Stop watching one television show a day and take a walk around the neighborhood.

Step 4: Keep a log of all food consumed, using paper or an app.

Do It Now!

DO IT NOW! That simple phrase can and will change your life. By using the mantra DO IT NOW!, you will be able to change a lifelong habit of procrastination. I began using this a decade ago. Consequently, I do not have dirty, cluttered cupboards, and my garage is always clean, neat, and orderly.

A great way to explain this is my suitcase. Before DO IT NOW!, after every trip my suitcase would make its way into my bedroom and stay there, open, lying on the floor for weeks. Now, regardless of what time I return home, I unpack my suitcase and put it away. It's amazing to have all my clothes back in the closet instead of staying in my suitcase. Doing this one chore immediately frees my time and my mind for more meaningful things.

By doing things now, you will be able to find the time for your relationships, your fitness goals, and your income goals. Three simple words will have an amazing impact on your life. They will keep you moving forward and not looking back at the past.

Dr. Clifford Lazarus says in "Beat Procrastination: DO IT NOW" (*Psychology Today*), "You can make motivation by taking action." It may sound odd, but it's true. Think about when there's a spot on the kitchen table. You clean it up and notice another. Suddenly you are cleaning the counter, then the floor and the cupboards. All of this happened because of one little spot on the counter. Taking the beginning step leads to another step, then another.

When you do things now, you complete the step without another one following. You can clean the spot on the kitchen table, and because everything else in the kitchen is cleaned, you move on. When you return to the kitchen, you won't have to stop and clean the spot on the table because it's already been done.

DO IT NOW! means what it says: DO IT NOW!. Don't wait for a more opportune time or a time when you feel like it. DO IT NOW!, and free yourself to achieve your goals.

If you are looking at eliminating your credit card debt, and with your current income it will take eight years to pay off that debt and you want to do it sooner, don't buy a lottery ticket. Maybe you need a second job. Think out of the box. If you have a day job, maybe you can start a cleaning company where you work at night and generate more income to help pay off the debt. This is an action step, a DO IT NOW! step.

DO IT NOW! requires action on your part. It is not about creating or believing. It is about performing an action right now, in the present. It is doing whatever comes in front of you, so you don't have to be concerned with it later.

Your first step is here. Read this, say it out loud, fifty times. Get it in your head. DO IT NOW!

Even Teenagers Can Stop Procrastinating

One of my friends has a teenage daughter who, like most teenagers, is a procrastinator supreme. She says that if there were a million dollars in front of her daughter, the daughter would procrastinate picking it up. This habit was the underlying reason for much uproar in the house. Then one day my friend put a sign on the fridge: *DO IT NOW!* She put one in the bathroom, one in the laundry room, one in her daughter's bedroom, and one by the back door. Everywhere the teenager turned, the sign said DO IT NOW. For the first couple of days, my friend reminded her daughter of the sign. When dinner was over and it was time to wash the dishes, she said, "DO IT NOW!" When the laundry basket was full, she said, "DO IT NOW!" When her daughter put a dish in the kitchen sink and not in the dishwasher, my friend said, "DO IT NOW!" After a couple of days, she noticed that she didn't have to say it as much, and everything was being done. Her daughter had changed her procrastination habit and replaced it with DO IT NOW!

My friend thought it would be more difficult, that there would be arguments or at least more resistance. But this wasn't the case. After a couple weeks she asked her daughter about DO IT NOW!

The daughter's response was, "If I get it done, then I'm free. It's really not that bad."

DO IT NOW! will change your life for the better. It will take you closer to your goals. You can do it. You *Believe It*.

Chapter Nine

KEEPING IT BALANCED

You don't have to be a fantastic hero to do certain things—to compete. You can be just an ordinary chap, sufficiently motivated to reach challenging goals.

— EDMUND HILLARY —

EVERY HOLIDAY SEASON *A Christmas Carol* appears on television. Ebenezer Scrooge is a character no one wants to be. Why is that? Is it because he's mean? Is it because he's greedy? Or is it because his life is so unbalanced, he isn't happy, and because he isn't happy, he makes everyone else miserable? It's all of these things, but the main problem connecting it all is imbalance. Once he is reminded of the error of his ways and focuses on more than just making money, he finds a balance in his life and becomes a better person.

I'm not saying that any one of you is Scrooge, but I am saying that most people do not live balanced lives.

There are hundreds of stories of businesspeople who neglect their family and get divorced. There are hundreds of stories of people so focused on climbing the career ladder that they neglect their health. Every one of you knows this story because it's your story or the story of someone you know.

A Value-Centered Life

Let's start with your values. Because many things require your attention every day, what you value the most can get lost in the barrage of information and demands. If you remember to keep your values in front, you will achieve more of what you value.

Think about what you value. If you value time with your family, being an "on-the-road" salesperson who's home only a few days each month may not be the best job for you. If you value free time on weekends, being on call on weekends wouldn't work for you. Of course, you also need to remember that having a job is the most important thing. But knowing what you value makes you aware of your choices and their consequences.

Eye on the Moneyball

Some of you might recognize the name Billy Beane—he was the general manager in the book *Moneyball: The Art of Winning an Unfair Game* and the subsequent movie *Moneyball*. He used statistics rather than conventional means to choose his players. After his success with the Oakland A's, he was offered a contract with the Boston Red Sox. He took the deal, then abruptly declined the offer. Why would he decline more money and more prestige with a storied club?

According to a story on NYTimes.com, Billy explained the decision: "I have a wife and kids and parents who all live out here," he said. "If it was strictly driven by the desire to just win games, and if that was the end-all for me, then yes. But this is the type of environment I like and enjoy." Or, as Bennett Miller, the director of *Moneyball*, put it: "He would have died in Boston. It wouldn't have been his show. He likes to be the guerrilla in the mountains in combat fatigues."

So what was important to Billy Beane wasn't money or prestige; it was family and the environment he worked in. His opportunity cost of leaving was a loss, while the opportunity cost of staying was a gain.

Opportunity Cost

One of the most famous adages in history is, "There ain't no such thing as a free lunch." In the 1800s it was common for saloons to offer a "free lunch" to anyone who had purchased at least one drink. A person could have as much as he wanted to eat, but the food was very salty, and the result was that the person would buy more and more drinks. The lunch itself was free, but the cost of the drinks added up to more than the cost of the food. The saloon made more money, and so the "free lunch" really wasn't so free.

The adage refers to the idea that it is impossible for a person to get something for nothing. It's true. Nothing comes without a cost, be it in money, in work, in being uncomfortable, or in opportunities lost.

Opportunity cost is defined by Investopedia.com as "the benefits you could have received by taking an alternative action." Another way to see it is to ask what you are giving up or gaining by making a choice. You may ask, "How does this apply to me?"

Suppose your goal is to lose weight, and you choose to eat a cookie rather than run two miles. What is the opportunity cost to you? It is a negative cost, because by eating the cookie you lost *and* by not running you lost. So you lost twice! If your choice is to not eat the cookie and to run the two miles, then you gain. A double gain! If you choose to run and then eat the cookie, the gain depends on the calories in the cookie. You do have a gain because you chose to run.

There is always an alternative to what you choose to do. It's determining what the difference is between the two choices that helps decide if the opportunity cost is a gain or loss.

You determine the cost of every choice you make. Each choice will either add to your success or take away from your success. For every choice you make, if it isn't positive, then it is a negative. Seldom, if ever, is it an even trade.

Calculating Opportunity Cost

When you look at opportunity cost in your life, you should balance it against your personal values. For example, if you have an opportunity to travel throughout the world for business, but your values lie with your family more than money, you would weigh that opportunity differently than someone who wants to travel and whose values are aligned with travel. That is, would travel be an asset or a liability for your balance sheet?

The assets on a balance sheet are equal to the liabilities plus the shareholder's equity (the investment you make in yourself as the largest stockholder in you, and the investment made by everyone in your life who has a share of your life stock). Investopedia.com explains, "It's called a balance sheet because the two sides balance out. This makes sense: a company has to pay for all the things it has (assets) by either borrowing money (liabilities) or getting it from shareholders (shareholders' equity).

The preceding definition defines liabilities in terms of money, whereas in your personal life stock it can be and always is more than just money.

EXERCISE: Your Life in Balance

Let's look at the opportunity cost of moving to North Dakota if you need a job.

First, fold a piece of paper in half lengthwise. Label the paper *PRO* on the left side and *CON* on the right side.

PRO   **CON**

_____   _____

_____   _____

_____   _____

_____   _____

_____   _____

The opportunity cost of moving to North Dakota becomes a positive. For every negative there is one or more corresponding positive(s). For example, consider moving away from family. You would now be able to call them and spend vacations with them. You would have the money to spend on things you can't afford now.

Financial Realism

Be realistic. Do you live paycheck to paycheck, or are you in a financial position to save money? If you live paycheck to paycheck, where are you going to get additional money? Should you get a second job? Should you sell items on eBay? You need to figure out how to get additional money, if savings is your goal and you do not make enough at one job to do more than live paycheck to paycheck.

If you are in a financial position to save, how much money can you save from your present position? Will that be enough for you to achieve your goal in a set period of time, or should you look at other financial opportunities?

This is why you have to be realistic. You can set a goal to "have one million dollars," but if you cannot achieve the goal, then it is no more than a false hope. If you are not willing to work to achieve the goal, then it is a false hope. Be realistic, be honest, and be willing to work.

If you say "I want to save money" and "I want to go on a cruise" in the same breath, what do you want? Do you want to save money, or do you want to go on a cruise? How can you discipline yourself to save money and go on a cruise? What is your priority? You have to know exactly what you want, so you can plan for it.

If you change your thoughts to, "I want to save money so I can go on a cruise," then you have the end in mind. You can discipline yourself to achieve the goal, because it is clear and concise. You can plan on exactly how much money you need to save. You can plan on how much time you will need. You can take specific steps to achieve your goal. You can monitor your progress, because you have a specific date you need to meet. You will know how much money per week you need to save. Because you have a specific goal in mind, you have what you need to make informed decisions and know the exact steps to take.

Fishing for Balance

An American businessman went for a holiday in Mexico. He watched a fisherman from his chair on the beach. When the fisherman approached, the businessman said, "That's a great catch. How long did it take you?"

The fisherman replied, "Not long."

The businessman asked, "Why didn't you stay longer and catch more fish?"

"Because this is enough for my family," the fisherman answered.

"What do you do with the rest of your day?" The businessman asked.

"I go home, play with my children, take a siesta, spend time with my wife. Then at night I go to town and spend time with my friends. I sing songs and enjoy their company. My life is full."

"If you stayed longer, you could catch more fish. Then you would make more money. You could buy a bigger boat, and keep making more money. One day you could own a plant and then you could move to the United States and have a big company."

"How long would that take?"

"About twenty-five to thirty years," the businessman answered.

"Then what?"

"Well then, you could sell the company and make millions of dollars," the businessman answered.

"What would I do then?"

"Then you could have fun. You could go back and live on the beach, do some fishing, play with your grandkids, take a siesta, and spend time with your wife. At night you could go to town with your friends, sing some songs, and have a good time."

The fisherman looked at the businessman as though he were crazy and walked away.

Life is about balance.

Chapter Ten

TAKING ADVANTAGE OF OPPORTUNITIES

The value of life lies not in the length of days,
but in the use we make of them.

— MICHEL DE MONTAIGNE —

EVERYTHING YOU DO, every action you take, will bring you forward. The only time you're not moving is when you are sitting down, afraid to move. Get up. Get moving.

Whatever your job is, whether it's parking cars, answering phones, or ringing up purchases, when you do it to the best of your ability and knowledge, when you strive to do it better than it's ever been done, you will move forward. You will be noticed and more opportunities will come your way.

Jobs that seem menial are the bedrock for those wanting to better themselves. You have to believe you can do anything and that means anything, including the most menial of tasks. You have to know a business from the bottom up if you are thinking about becoming a manager of a team. If you don't understand what you are asking of someone, how will you know if it's being done correctly? You have to keep working.

Answer the Phone

In order to get the opportunities coming to you, you must answer the phone. When you realize and decide what you truly want, the universe will align and the opportunities will come to you. If you don't take the calls, you're going to miss them and they will skip right by you.

Imagine you're thinking one night about how you're ready to lose weight. You get all revved up about what you're going to do tomorrow. The next day you have the opportunity to win a free membership to the gym. But if you don't answer the phone, you don't get it. *Answer the phone!*

Of course this is just an imaginary story, but if you think of "answering the phone" as a metaphor for how you accept the opportunities always coming to you, then you will see the bigger picture. If one day, a friend tells you that her company is hiring and you need a job, *answer the phone*. It's the universe calling and telling you what you should do. If you are losing weight and someone tells you they have a bumper crop of veggies that need a home, *answer the phone*. The universe is calling and telling you about healthy foods. Believe it or not, there is no answering service that takes the place of answering the phone. It's an all-or-nothing thing. Don't let your voice mail keep you from getting what you want. Answer the phone and stay in the present.

Unemployed to App Empire

In 2009 Chad Mureta owned a successful real estate agency in South Carolina. While he was driving home from a basketball game his car hit a deer, flipping the car and crushing his left arm. After two major surgeries and an eighteen-month recuperation, he found himself drowning in over $100,000 in medical bills and unable to return to work. While in the hospital he read a magazine article about mobile apps and, needing a new income stream, decided to start an app business. Not having any education in the business other than what he had read, he began to come up with ideas and found a development company to create his vision. His first app made him over $140,000 and led him to build his app empire, consisting of over forty-six apps that have been downloaded over thirty-five million times. His book, *App Empire: Make Money, Have a Life, and Let Technology Work for You*, was released in 2012. Mureta credits his success to his being able to take advantage of an opportunity that presented itself.

Moving Up

Rachel started working for my company as a receptionist. I'd never even met her, as I didn't personally hire her. She did so well at her job that when a position in our scheduling department opened, she applied for the job and got it. She excelled at the job and soon thereafter became the manager of the department. Everyone soon knew, "If you want something done, give it to Rachel." She did everything well, from getting back to someone to running personal errands. She was willing to do whatever it took to move up in the company. Her pay increased, her abilities increased, she took courses to assist her in management and leadership, and then she took the initiative to get those classes for her team. Her leadership skills expanded and she was promoted to managing two departments. Today she is the operations manager.

What Are You Sitting on Right Now?

Once there was a man sitting by the side of the road. He was in dirty clothes and asking for money. A wealthy man passed him and took pity. He owned the land where the man sat, so he stopped and said, "I will give you an acre of this ground." The ground was full of fruit trees that produced beautiful fruit. People would come from near and far to purchase the fruit from this orchard. The poor man accepted the gift.

About a year later the wealthy man went by the orchard and saw that all the trees had been cut down. What was once a beautiful productive orchard was now a barren piece of ground. The poor man again sat by the side of the road begging for money. The wealthy man stopped and asked what had happened to the fruit trees. The poor man replied, "I cut them down and sold the wood."

The wealthy man shook his head. "Didn't you know that the fruit trees would give fruit and make you much money every year?" The poor man shook his head and said, "I didn't notice. I've always sold wood."

Are you aware of what is around you? Think of what opportunities you may be sitting on and never noticed were there. Again, whatever you focus on, you will see.

EXERCISE: Uncovering Opportunities

The average American watches over 34 hours of live television a week and then watches an additional 4–6 hours of taped programs. That breaks down to about 5½ hours a day. Here's my question to you: how many hours of TV do you watch a day?

Write it down: _____

What COULD you be doing instead of watching TV?

Here are some ideas:

- Spend more time with family

- Learn a new language

- Start a business

- Work out more

- Continue your education

- Read more

- Perform charitable work

Now write down what you will do when you watch TV for only one hour a day. What will you accomplish?

Let's think about uncovering your opportunities. What will happen if you lose weight?

How many pounds do you want to lose?

Write it down: _____

What COULD you do if you lost weight? Here are some examples:

- Be healthier

- Wear smaller size clothes

- Run a marathon

- Improve my tennis game

- Ride bikes with my family

- Fit comfortably in an airline seat

Now write down what you will do when you lose weight. What will you accomplish? _____

_____

_____

Really Be Okay with Uncomfortable

We talked about the concept of being uncomfortable with regard to procrastination earlier . . . why you shouldn't put things off because they will only get harder to tackle as the dragons get bigger in your mind. Well, guess what: having a habit of making yourself uncomfortable will come in real handy when you are faced with an opportunity that scares you a little or asks more of you than you previously thought possible.

Many people live by the adage "It's better to live with the devil you know than the one you don't." This means that it is better to deal with a person or thing you know, even if you do not like them, than to deal with a new person or thing that could be even worse. That is the mindset of someone who will never go forward because she is complacent about where she is now. She believes it's okay to be miserable because it might get even more miserable somewhere else. Hogwash! You have to believe it will get better. You have to believe that being uncomfortable for a while will bring great results in the future. Take that step. Take that leap of faith.

Make yourself uncomfortable. Try new things. Go out on a limb. Take the risk. Ride that bike! You will adapt and you will learn. And most importantly, you will learn to believe.

If you're comfortable, you are NOT growing!

If you're growing, you are NOT comfortable!

Lucille Ball, the famous comedian and actress, once said, "I'd rather regret the things I've done than regret the things I haven't done."

Live your life to its fullest, take care of the things you need to, make yourself uncomfortable, and you will reap great rewards.

Think about the things that have made you uncomfortable in the past, like your first job interview or the first time riding a bike without training wheels.

When most kids first lose the training wheels on their bikes, they have a moment or two of being unsteady; they may even crash a time or two. But the lure of riding the bike like a big kid, without those training wheels, propels them into trying again and again. They have the desire to be great at bike riding. They don't care how many times they fall or wobble; they just keep getting back on the bike until they can ride like the wind. By being uncomfortable for a period of time, they achieve freedom. The uncomfortable part is forgotten once the rewards come through.

Remember your first job interview. If you're like most people, you were up half the night before, it took hours to make sure you looked right, and you spent time in your car or on the bus on the way to the interview feeling like you were going to puke. You were uncomfortable while you waited for the interview, and you were nervous during the interview, but when you were through, relief set in. You made it through in one piece.

By doing both of these uncomfortable things, you moved your life moved forward in a positive direction. You learned that you were capable of riding a bike and of presenting yourself as a candidate for a job. Nothing new is ever comfortable. We get set in our habits, in what our status quo is, even if it's miserable.

Go Where You Need to Go

Everything in life requires that you set your mind to it and believe it. When there are no jobs in your area, you may need to open yourself up to moving to where jobs are. With every economic turn, jobs open up in certain areas. It could be oil shale in rural Utah or a new company in Texas.

Let me guess—you don't like the idea of moving, or it's not convenient. You're asking, "Who would want to move?" That's simple. People who need jobs; that's who.

If you're in a city where there aren't a lot of jobs, you have to expand your mind. Be open to where getting a job is going to take you, and accept that it may involve relocating. Get practical about the opportunities in the area where you live. If they aren't there, look around.

"But if we move, my kids will be in a different school and have different friends!" you might say. I say, "Would you rather have that or have them on the street?" You've got to be realistic about things. So many times people are looking for the perfect job. But here's the deal. The perfect job is the one that gives you a paycheck to cash every payday—and when you cash that check, it doesn't bounce. That's the perfect job at that time.

Whatever job you have, if you're the best at it, it's going to open other doors. It always does. That's not just true sometimes or part of the time. *It's true all the time.* Keep working every day to make yourself better at what you do. Keep working every day to take another step or two toward your goal. Keep working whether or not you "feel like it." If you do, you will find success. The universe will bring it to you, and not through a fairy godmother. It will come because you earned it and worked for it.

Chapter Eleven

POSITIVE ATTITUDE

Everything negative—pressure, challenges—
is all an opportunity for me to rise.

— KOBE BRYANT —

ONE DAY an old mule fell down the farmer's well. He began to bray and in time the farmer and some neighbors came over to see what all the noise was about. Everyone looked into the well and then sat together to figure out the solution. After hours of discussion they decided the best tack was to simply bury the mule to put him out of his misery. As the first shovel of dirt fell on the mule's back he panicked. Over and over the shovels of dirt fell on the poor mule's back. Then the mule figured it out. With every shovel of dirt, the hole became shallower. All he had to do was stay on top of the dirt. He would shake it off and climb again. Time and time again the shovels of dirt pounded his back and time and time again, he shook it off and climbed a bit higher. Finally he was able to get out of the well. What should have buried him alive became his salvation.

Life is lived above the earth, not six feet under. When someone asks you, "How are you doing?" and your reply is, "Just surviving," that's what you'll get out of life. Just survival. You will never see anything but pain and agony in your life.

When I'm asked, "How are you doing?" my answer is swift: "I'm living the dream." I then get asked, "Are you always living the dream?"

My answer: "What's the alternative?" I don't want to be six feet under.

You control whether your attitude is positive or negative. It's your choice how you respond to what happens to you. It's an "Is the glass half full or half empty?" thought process. If you see the glass as half empty, you're looking at it in a negative way. A glass half full is positive. You have the power to put things in a positive way, regardless of the situation.

Say things in a positive way. Believe your life is great because your life is great. How you speak determines whether your glass is half empty or half full. Tell the world your glass is half full. Let everyone, including yourself, know that, because it's your truth!

Show Up Positive or Stay Home!

The first step for those of you currently employed is to be the very best at what you do. Go in to work every day with a good positive attitude. When I'm speaking to groups, I ask them, "How many of you had to drag yourself out of bed to come to work today? How many of you said to yourself, 'I don't want to go to work. I hate my job. I don't like what I do or the people I work with. I don't want to go.' My answer to you is "Do us all a favor and *stay home*! No one wants your negativity! You're going to bring all of us down. If you don't want to be here, don't come!"

That's the best thing you can do. Stay home and get your mind right. Prepare yourself to be the very best at what you do. If you shovel manure, be the best manure shoveler. If you clean toilets, clean them better than anyone else. If you answer phones, answer phones better than anyone else. One of my favorite things to do is call companies and see how they answer the phone. You can learn a lot about a company by the way they answer their phone.

Kolby, who works at our hair school, answers the phone better than anyone I've seen at any company. We trained him to do it correctly, but the passion he has when he answers the phone is amazing. Does Kolby always want to answer the phones that way? NO! He has challenges and pains like everyone else, but he decides when he wakes up every morning that he is going to focus on positivity and answer the phone the right way. He knows that in order to be a "day maker," and make someone's day on the other end of the phone, he has to answer with enthusiasm. He doesn't know who's on the other line. It could be the president of the United States or someone who wants a pedicure. It doesn't matter because he answers the phone the right way every time.

Get the Ice Cream

Be the best at whatever you do and you will enhance your value. Then, as we covered in Chapter Seven, dollars will follow. When people say they're not getting paid what they're worth, maybe the truth is they would be paid more if they had a better attitude.

Those of you with children will know this situation well. When your child acts whiny and demands ice cream, he doesn't get any because you don't want to give it to a whiny child. When your child says, "I love you so much. Can we get some ice cream?" Odds are, you get her ice cream. It's not just being a sucker for your kids; it's about rewarding them for the correct behavior.

If you are a whiny employee, finding fault, complaining, and dwelling in the basement of negativity, you won't get ice cream. Kids have a lot to teach us about the real world. Be the employee who is positive all of the time and doesn't whine. You will end up with the ice cream.

Just remember, dollars follow value. When you are the best at what you do, someone will recognize it. You may move up in the company you work for, or someone outside your current company may recognize your positive work ethic and commitment to excellence. Every single time your attitude will be recognized and you will get more opportunities than you know what to do with. If it doesn't happen today, it will tomorrow. It will happen. You just have to be there to reap the rewards.

You Always Have a Choice

In any situation where you receive information, you have a choice to react or respond. When you react it's because of emotion, and that's not a good choice. The adage "When emotions are high, intelligence is low" is true. When your body reacts to a medication, that's not positive.

When your body responds to a medication, that's positive. You need to respond to any situation. When you respond, it's you who is in control, not your emotions. When you take the time to become aware of what is going on, you make a conscious choice. Ambrose Bierce once said, "Speak when you are angry and you will make the best speech you will ever regret."

Every question, every situation has an answer and an alternative answer. Every feeling has an alternative feeling. You choose: misery or happiness? Excitement or dullness? It's always your choice. Dirt falls on everyone. It's how you manage the dirt that determines your future. When you don't feel that you're approaching a situation with the right answer, ask yourself, what's the alternative?

What's the Alternative?

Muji Karim had a choice to make, a choice between choosing to live a life of quality or living a life of despair. Muji Karim was an elite athlete, a starter for the University of New Hampshire's football team, and his athletic prowess and toned body brought him great rewards. Everything changed one night when he and his brother were involved in an auto accident. He had third-degree burns on both legs and on his left hand, and he was given a 10 to 20 percent chance of living. He was knocked unconscious in the accident and when he woke from a coma three weeks later, a nurse broke the news to him that both of his legs had been amputated. When he thought of the impact of losing his legs he said, "It was tough. It was just all sort of surreal."

There were times, especially at the beginning, when he thought death might have been a better option than what he had. But those times passed because as he says, "I'm more of a glass half full kind of guy."

He made a conscious choice against being defined by his injuries and against being known as the guy who played football and then lost his legs. He chose to stay who he was inside, both before and after the accident. Muji's rehabilitation was tough, but he pushed through it and he can now walk with prosthetics. There were a thousand reasons why he could have given up, a thousand reasons to not try. In the end, he chose to live a meaningful and full life. He had the choice of an alternative life, a potentially miserable one, but he chose a great life. We all have a choice.

Never Give Up, Never Give In

The year 2012 was heralded as the year Michael Phelps would break the all-time Olympic medal record. There was no doubt that his first event would be the beginning of great things. But it didn't turn out that way. For the first time since 2000 Michael Phelps failed to medal. At that point the newspaper headlines read *Michael Phelps fails to medal*, *Lochte beats Michael Phelps*, and *Without burning desire, Michael Phelps flames out*. The skeptics stood in line waiting for the story of failure. They were to be disappointed.

After that event, Michael Phelps won six more medals, surpassing records for both most all-time gold medals ever won as well as most medals ever won by one athlete in the Olympic Games.

Michael Phelps did not let one disappointing result derail him from his goal of becoming the most decorated Olympic athlete. He did not have the "perfect" Olympics, but he accomplished what he set out to do. He didn't need perfection to achieve his goal. He just had to believe that his hard work would propel him over the top.

Chapter Twelve

FOLLOWING FOOTPRINTS

Success always leaves footprints.

— Booker T. Washington —

Success always leaves footprints. I first learned this lesson when I was in high school and on the wrestling team. We had a new student, Josh, move into our school, and he was just unbelievable. This dude could do anything he wanted on the wrestling mat. He'd been working on and perfecting a takedown move called the outside single shot. The outside single shot requires a series of moves performed in a specific order, mostly using his outside leg.

Because of this, I had a set of footprints to follow, and I wanted to be like Josh. I followed the steps he'd set, and I became known as the outside single guy, the mini Josh. I would watch Josh take someone down with the single leg, and I'd do all the same moves to take someone down the same way.

I'd determined that I wanted to be like Josh and be able to use the outside single leg move, so I did. If Josh hadn't been there as my mentor and left his footsteps for me to follow, I might have chosen another move, from another mentor.

Every successful person knows there are no secrets to success. Every successful person I have ever met has been willing to show me how he accomplished his goals when I asked. One of the qualities of successful people is that they help to develop others who want to learn. They share their knowledge, network with others, and genuinely want everyone to be their best. By doing so they continue to learn from others as they help others. They work as part of a team, always pulling their own weight while showing others the way to success.

Every successful person has done something that will resonate in you. They have achieved success. It may be that they express it in different words, in different ways, or in different fields than you, but nonetheless they have experienced achieving success, and you can and should learn from them.

Success is more than achieving one goal. It is more than one event. It is an attitude you carry with you. It is the knowledge that you believe you can do anything because you can and will work to achieve it. You *Believe It*!

The Greats Were Inspired by Others, Too

Athletes look for inspiration in those who came before, be it generations or years. There are careers to follow or records to beat. By nature, an athlete is competitive and strives to be the best. When there are clear goals, like beating a shooting percentage or winning ten gold medals, athletes are always acutely aware of where they are in relationship to their goals.

Let's look at Tiger Woods, who dreamed and believed he would become the greatest golfer in history. Ever since Tiger was a youngster, he kept a timeline of all Jack Nicklaus's milestones. Step by step he plotted his career choices, using the track of Jack Nicklaus. Following the path required hard work and dedication. It wasn't just the fact that he knew each individual accomplishment Jack had made; he also had to learn how to achieve each step to complete every individual goal. Doing that alone required hard work. It took tenacity and an unending will to achieve success. But because it had been done before him, he could readily believe it was possible, and he had footprints to follow in his journey. He believed he could, because Jack Nicklaus had already done it.

Michael Phelps had the footprints of Mark Spitz to follow. In an interview he said, "What [Mark Spitz] did is an amazing feat. Being able to have something to shoot for, it made those days when you were tired and didn't want to work out, it made those days easier, to look at him and say, 'I want to do this.' I'm thankful for having him do what he did."

Once Michael beat Mark Spitz's record, his goal was to earn more career Olympic medals than anyone in history. Soviet gymnast Larisa Latynina held the record of eighteen career medals, winning her last in the 1964 Olympics. Michael surpassed this by winning twenty-two career Olympic medals.

What you can see is that his goal was more than just beating the swimmer with the most medals; it was beating the Olympian with the most medals. Footprints for success can be found anywhere, and as you achieve one goal, another should take its place.

Inspiration Flows Two Ways

The thing about inspiration is that it can be a two-way street. Such is the story of Tim Tebow and Jacob Rainey, as reported by ESPN.

Jacob Rainey, a highly rated high school quarterback in Virginia, was a competitor. During a routine scrimmage in his junior year, his right knee was dislocated. While hospitalized, he learned that the artery in his knee had been severed and he'd lost all blood supply to the leg. Over the next week, he underwent four surgeries to repair the blood supply, and all were unsuccessful. A week after the scrimmage, his right leg was amputated above the knee.

In Rainey's words, "After the procedure and I saw it, that is when it really hit me. I just broke down and cried. I was just like, 'I don't know how I'm going to come back from this.'"

Enter Alabama football coach Nick Saban, Green Bay Packers linebacker Clay Matthews, and Denver Broncos quarterback Tim Tebow, who wished Jacob well. But Tim Tebow went one step further. "It's hard for me to even imagine something like that," Tebow said. "For Jacob working for something so hard and having a dream being so close to coming true, then falling short, is something that is very tough to deal with. I heard what he went through, everything he was going through at the time. I said, 'Let's find a way to be able to encourage him.'"

And encourage he did. On December 24, 2011, Jacob Rainey, his father, and his older brother attended a Broncos game as Tebow's guests. That meeting inspired Jacob toward a new goal: to play quarterback again. Over the next few months he tried out different prosthetic legs. Many didn't work, but then he found a motor-knee used by snowboarders and motocross racers. Not only was he able to throw a football, but he earned the starting quarterback position a year after the accident.

Tebow and Rainey had stayed in touch, and on the day of the game, Tebow sent this text message: *Hey Jacob, this is tebow. Would love to catch up sometime. Been hearing a lot of great stuff about u!!! I know tonight is a big night so congrats! I'm praying for u and here if u ever need anything! Stay blessed my friend!*

Three games into the season, Rainey threw his first touchdown pass of the season.

Tebow's take on Jacob Rainey? "It's awe-inspiring. It's something that I think can be an inspiration to people all over the country."

Be Someone Else's Inspiration

One of my friends, Sandra, lives in the Avenues area of Salt Lake City, Utah. This neighborhood boasts coffee shops and restaurants within walking distance of her home. Years ago, Sandra adopted a little girl of a different race, and together they frequented the local shops. All during her daughter's preschool years, they could be seen every morning getting a hot chocolate at the local coffee shop. For a while, they were regulars, and the barista who worked there knew what they wanted before they even ordered. Eventually, as Sandra's daughter entered school, they went to the coffee shop less and less.

Years later, when Sandra's daughter was a teenager, a visitor came to Sandra's door. She asked if Sandra remembered her, but she didn't. Then the woman said, "I was the barista at the coffee shop many years ago. I used to watch you and your daughter. You looked so happy together. I live a couple blocks away and I've watched your daughter ride her bike by my house. She's grown into a beautiful young lady. I want you to know that I adopted my daughter a couple months ago. It was a long process but the memory of you and your daughter inspired me to keep at it. I just want to thank you."

Sandra congratulated her. Sandra had never given any thought to inspiring someone to choose adoption. She just lived her life the way she chose, never realizing how by doing so she was an inspiration to others.

By living your life you will be inspiring others. You may not know it now, you may find out later, or maybe you'll never know. But one thing is certain. When you live a life full of belief, you will inspire someone.

Inspiration in Real Time (and Real Life)

What about in "real life"? You don't know about any record to beat in the accounting world or as a city worker. How do you find the footprints, or blueprints, if you prefer, for where you want to go?

First, choose someone who is successful. Research them, read their books, find them on social media, follow their tweets. As you do this, you will find even more people who have succeeded, probably some in your area, and you can learn about them, why they succeed, how they do it. Use these people as your mentors. Ask them questions. See if they have volunteer opportunities you can access. Pay attention to what they post or what questions they ask.

As you do this, you will learn about them and discover what you like and what you don't. You can take what you want and leave the rest. For example, say you find a business entrepreneur who is extremely successful. As you research his life, you find that his personal life is in shambles and his reputation is not aligned with your values. That's okay. Find the things he does that work for you. Then research another person, and take what he or she has to give. This is a critical step in achieving success. You don't need to reinvent the wheel. You have more important things to do with your life.

In order to make choices about what to take, you must be aware of who you are and exactly what you want to accomplish. You may find, through your research, that you want to expand your goals—if so, great. Do it. If someone else has accomplished it, there is a path for you to follow.

It is crucial that you believe that you can do it. You have to be able to look in the mirror and say, "I am going to achieve my goals and I Believe It." It is all about believing you can do it.

If you want to get down to 12 percent body fat, then it's about you looking in the mirror with conviction and saying, "I have 12 percent body fat." You absolutely have to believe that. Whatever the goal is, you have to believe it. Your goals are in the present, not in the future. You need to see yourself in the present as having achieved the goal.

Once you find your mentor or mentors, then you need to look at yourself. What skills do you already have and what skills do you need to develop? How will you learn new skills? Make a plan and then follow it. If you model your life after someone who has incredible speaking skills and you are not comfortable with public speaking, you need to make a plan. Join Toastmasters, take a class, and practice in your mirror. Create opportunities for yourself to learn the skills you need.

No One's Perfect

When you are looking for your path to follow, one of the important steps is to see how your "mentor" has handled setbacks. How were they able to overcome mistakes and use the experience to grow? Every single person who is successful has felt the pain of failure. On the road to success, they failed, probably more than once. Learn from them how to move on, how to persevere, and maintain confidence in yourself when things don't go the way you planned. It's going to happen, so prepare yourself for what is to come.

What you need to know is that someone before you has found a way to achieve what you want. Even if you want to build a prototype engine, remember, someone else has invented something that once had never been seen before. It is possible—and when you Believe It, it will happen.

Amelia Earhart is known as a pioneer. She is the inspiration for many who followed after her. What few people realize is that she kept a scrapbook filled with newspaper clippings of successful women in predominantly male-dominated careers such as the law, film direction and production, mechanical engineering, and management and advertising.

None of these women were aviators, but they were successful and left footprints for her to follow. So even before women were known for their aviation skills, Amelia Earhart found successful women and patterned her life after theirs.

It is key that you have a path to follow. You must go out and find the path for you. Remember, success leaves footprints.

EXERCISE: Who Inspires You?

Think of the people who inspire you. What is it about them that you find inspiring? Could it be you have those same qualities, and that's why you are drawn to those particular things? Work on those qualities inside you.

Now, think about the people you might inspire. You would be surprised just how many people it could be.

Crack Your Own Egg

While I was at my grandfather's farm one spring, all of the kids brought baby chick and baby duck eggs into the house and put them under a light to watch them hatch. The baby chicks were cracking their eggs without any problem, but there was a baby duckling that was struggling to crack its shell. A small crack would appear and then another but not enough to allow the baby to break through the shell. It kept trying and trying and I decided to just take a bit of shell off to give it some help. Still the duckling did not emerge and I took a bit more of the shell out and helped the baby out of its prison. It was the cutest little duckling ever. The next morning I went back to see the baby and it was dead. It was no longer weak; it was dead! I asked one of my uncles what happened, and he told me that the baby duckling had to crack through the shell on its own so it would be strong enough to live. In my attempts to help the baby, I had unwittingly stolen its life. I still remember that little duckling and the lesson it taught me. Don't take away the things that make others stronger.

It's hard to watch people we love face trials. We want to step in and help them, but that's not necessarily the best for them. What is important is to be there, in the present, cheering them on and telling them they can get through it. It's the same for each of us. We all appreciate having a cheerleader rooting for us, not doing our work, but just cheering us on. As parents we want to give our kids all the things we didn't have. All the things we worked so hard to get, we think we should give to them. That's not helping. It's not fair to crack their eggs. They have to do it themselves so they are tough enough to succeed throughout their lives, not just today.

Why do you think there are so many first-generation millionaires? It's because they had to work for success, because it wasn't given to them. How many trust fund babies go on to build financial empires? Approximately 80 percent of all millionaires are first generation, and typically the second and third generation will decimate the fortune. The second generation hasn't had to work. They haven't felt the pain of not having what others have.

Everything they want is already there. Did they crack their own egg? They, like the baby duckling I thought I was helping, will not have had the opportunity to grow strong, to grow resilient.

A Word about Your Children

It's hard to let your children make mistakes and then deal with the consequences of the mistakes. We tell our children that mistakes are just another way to learn, but as parents, our actions say something else. "While we do not want our children to face ongoing failure to attempt to overprotect them and rush in whenever we fear they may fail at a task, robs them of the important lesson, namely that mistakes are experiences from which to learn," write Robert Borks and Sam Goldstein, two prominent child-development experts. "It also communicates another subtle or perhaps not-so-subtle message to a child: 'We don't think you are strong enough to deal with obstacles and mistakes.'"

Kids are resilient. They learn and grow from their mistakes. They have to make mistakes in order to grow.

In Michael Jordan's Hall of Fame speech, he talks about his love of basketball and the joy and pain it brought him.

"The game of basketball has been everything to me. My refuge. My place I've always gone when I needed to find comfort and peace. It's been a source of intense pain, and a source of most intense feelings of joy and satisfaction. And one that no one can even imagine. It's been a relationship that has evolved over time, and given me the greatest respect and love for the game. It has provided me with a platform to share my passion with millions in a way I neither expected nor could have imagined in my career. I hope that it's given the millions of people that I've touched, the optimism and the desire to achieve their goals through hard-work, perseverance, and positive attitude."

What if someone had stepped in and kept Michael Jordan from feeling the pain that came along with the joy of basketball? Would he have succeeded? Would he have reached the heights he did? Michael Jordan became arguably the best basketball player ever, in part because he cracked his own egg.

Chapter Thirteen

DEALING WITH CHANGE

Always in motion is the future.

— YODA —

N O ONE EVER has a perfect day. Every day things happen that are out of your control. People say things; random acts occur. All of these things happen every day. All of these things are there, floating above you, waiting to detonate. If you choose to pull them down and hold them close to your heart, they will explode and you will suffer. If you choose to let them detonate above you, because they really aren't that important to you, you are not gravely injured. It doesn't mean there isn't fallout. Of course there is. What it does mean is that you can deal with fallout; what's hard to deal with is something exploding in your face. You choose what to accept into your life.

I was working with a life coach and one day, just before my session, I was given the devastating news that my grandfather had died. This shook me to the core and I fell on my knees. He meant the world to me and I had no idea how I would go on without the benefit of his love and knowledge. I shared my devastation with my life coach, and she said to me, "What was your gift in this?" I was speechless. She obviously hadn't heard the news correctly. I repeated that my life was shattered. She was silent for a moment, then asked again, "What was your gift in this?" I was dumbstruck. Having nothing to say, all I could do was try to hear what she was saying. Then it hit me—there was another side. I'd had the gift of my grandfather, his love, and his knowledge. Because of his teaching, I knew how to go on. Then I found gratitude. I was grateful for my grandfather. I was grateful for his love and his knowledge.

Remembering my grandfather didn't diminish the pain I felt from losing him. It didn't change the fact that he was no longer with me. What gratitude did for me was remind me of the wonderful gifts that for my entire life my grandfather had bestowed on me. It allowed me to celebrate the life of a man I admired and loved. It kept me from seeing only what I'd never have again, to seeing all the time I *did* have with him. No matter what adversity comes your way, you must remember there is a lesson in it because, just like the duck in the egg, we all need adversity and trials to make us stronger.

Use Change to Your Advantage

The one guarantee you have in life is that things never stay the same. You already know the importance of maintaining a positive attitude for success. Remember, whatever life throws at you, you have the choice to respond or react. You always have a choice.

The farmer is well aware of how quickly things can change, and because of this, he stays focused on his job. The Law of the Harvest demands that the farmer be attuned to his land; the weather; the temperature conditions; the changing water levels; and the types of seed, insects, and growth patterns. Just because he plants the seed doesn't mean it's guaranteed to grow. Planting the seed is the first of many continual steps a farmer must take.

In your life, it's no different. You've planted the seed. You believe in yourself. You believe you can have anything you want as long as you work for it. That's just the beginning, a seed. In order for the seed to grow, to thrive, you must be willing not only to accept change but also to learn to use it to your advantage.

You need to realize and accept that change is inevitable. It will happen either quickly or slowly, but it will happen. Nothing ever stays the same, ever. You cannot control what does and does not change; all you can do is manage how you deal with change.

Because of Mother Nature's fickle ways, farmers must become

comfortable with change. They know the wisdom of preparedness, and they take steps to prepare for the worst using such techniques as integrative pest management. But being prepared can't account for everything. Farmers know that a hailstorm can wipe out a crop and there is nothing they can do to prevent it. They know that an infestation of insects can decimate a field and there is nothing they can do to stop it. They know that a lightning strike can cause an animal to die and there is nothing they can do to prevent it. Being a farmer demands that you prepare yourself as you best you can, but that you also cultivate the skill of accepting and dealing with change. And that, too, is a type of preparedness.

It's not always so black and white when you're not a farmer. Most people don't worry about whether a hailstorm will destroy their living, or a bolt of lightning will kill their best brood mare. But there is really no difference between the farmer and the urban dweller. Change is inevitable in all of life at any time. You better be prepared to deal with it.

Be Prepared for Changing Opportunities

Part of dealing with change is being emotionally and mentally prepared to respond in a positive way no matter what happens, even when change disappoints you. If you can do this, you will more easily spot the new opportunities that may reveal themselves. Sometimes things happen that we don't expect, but that doesn't mean it's for the worst.

Consider the story of Tony Beltran, who plays professional soccer with Real Salt Lake in Major League Soccer (MLS). Before this opportunity came along, he was an amateur player who worked hard to achieve success. When he was nineteen years old, he had an opportunity to try out for the United States Under 20 World Cup Team. Here is the story in his words from Beyond the Net:

"I remember I was called into the camp for the U20 World Cup. There were thirty-plus players going to camp, but only eighteen or twenty actually go to the qualifying tournaments. You are there for three weeks and you train. The cuts come two days before the last day. Get cut—go home. The people who make it go to qualifying and a place on the World Cup team. The second-to-last day I was let go, I was cut. I didn't think I deserved to be cut. Obviously I believe in myself and I want to be there. I love representing my country, love putting on that shirt. It was a huge disappointment. On the last day, the day after the cuts, they were doing fitness. Everyone who got cut asked for early flights home and got out of there. I decided to stay and continue and finish out the camp, finish what I started. I talked to my dad that night on the phone and explained to him how I felt. He gave me advice, and we both decided that this was the right thing to do, even though I didn't make it.

"I was really good at fitness and gave it all I had. There was nothing to lose, no pressure the next day. I remember the coach talking to me after and being like 'It's a big sign of character staying out here, so if someone gets hurt you are going to be the first alternate to be called up.' Someone did in fact get hurt. I remember it was New Year's Day when they called me and said, 'You're going to Panama. Pack your bags. You're leaving in two days.' I was so excited, and I ended up starting every game in the qualifying (rounds) and every game in the World Cup."

Tony Beltran went on to be chosen as one of only eleven Adidas Generation players for the MLS in 2008. He plays professional soccer and has been chosen as a member of the United States National Team numerous times.

Be a Phoenix

The mythical phoenix is a bird that lives in constant flux. At the end of its life, the phoenix returns to its nest, where it settles in and bursts into flame. Both the phoenix and the nest perish. Then the miraculous thing happens, and a fledgling phoenix rises from the ashes to begin again. It is the death of the old phoenix that gives emergence to a new phoenix.

The legend of the phoenix flows through different cultures and countries and goes by different names. But the basic concept—dying and starting again fresh—is constant. The phoenix represents letting go of what you cannot control and beginning again under new circumstances. The phoenix represents the power of personal change: the power you hold inside you.

Every time there is change, you grow. It may not be the way you expected or a way you embrace, but nonetheless, as change happens, you change also. You can fight it or you can learn the skills of dealing with change. It's up to you. It's always your choice.

All around you are people who embrace change. They're the ones always moving forward, never stopping to look back and say, "If only." These are the phoenixes. These are the people who have the skills you need. Watch them and see how they come through even the hottest of fires with great attitudes and forward thinking.

One of the key concepts in dealing with change is to admit, "You don't know what you don't know." No one knows everything, including you. So much of life is out of your control: how people act, how they react, the inevitabilities of life and death. These are things you cannot know, cannot control, cannot predict, and cannot change. Accept them.

However, you can control how you accept change and how you act. Notice I didn't say react; I said act. Take control of your life. Choose how you deal with change.

When you're faced with hard situations, you have opportunities to grow. And so you can either put your head in the sand and curl up in a little ball and let the situation hurt you, or you can become innovative, embrace it, and say, "Okay, how can we get better?"

Having gone through a hard time and having to change means your knowledge base is greater than it was before, right? Sometimes the best lessons that we have are when we have to crack our own egg, when we do have to go through adversity and pick ourselves up by the bootstraps and go forth. And knowing that you've gone through that gives you a new advantage.

It's not easy going through hard times. No healthy person ever chooses pain and suffering, but you will experience both in your life. These things happen to every single person. The only way to move forward is to work through them and come out stronger on the other side.

The phoenix is reborn through fire. Be a phoenix.

Resilient Like a Rubber Band

It seems when disaster strikes there are always people who do the right things. They do what others won't. They do or say things that others should, but don't. What makes them different from the others? Were they born with something special? Didn't they have to face hardship in the past? Odds are, they did face hardship, just like anyone else. What makes them different from most is how they choose to deal with their emotions during the hardship. They choose not to be victims and to act rather than react. Being resilient is a skill that can be learned.

Dictionary.com defines resilience is defined as "being able to recoil or spring back into shape after bending, stretching or being compressed. Able to withstand or quickly recover from difficult situations."

Resilience is a necessary part of following the Law of the Harvest. There isn't anything in life that always goes the way we plan, the way we hope. Things will keep coming up, and it's up to you to be able to find a way to be resilient while still moving forward toward your goals.

Being resilient means staying in the solution to the problem and not wallowing in the problem. If all you see is the problem and never choose to look for or see the solution, then you remain stuck where you are. You can't possibly be successful if you choose to remain a victim of your circumstances. But because you are not a victim, you can and will find a solution to the problem before you.

People have certain skills that make them resilient. These include a positive attitude, optimism, and the ability to control their emotions and see failure as a type of feedback, not as an end. No matter what misfortune may happen to people with these skills, they are able to overcome any obstacle and find the solution.

127 Hours

Aron Ralston is a hiker who became the subject of the movie *127 Hours*. While he was hiking the slot canyons in southern Utah, his right hand got pinned against the slot canyon wall, and he couldn't free it. He was stuck for many days. By the fifth day he was out of food and water and, because he had not told anyone where he was hiking, he knew no one would be looking for him. He had to make the decision to cut off his own arm to survive. Even amputating his arm would not guarantee his survival, because he would still have to deal with the blood loss and hike eight miles back to his car to get help.

Aron did amputate his forearm with a dull multitool knife after he had broken his radius and ulna. He accomplished this by using torque against his trapped arm, because he had no way to saw through the bones unless they were already broken. He did all of this on his own without any type of medical assistance.

Once freed, he had to hike the eight miles back to his car. Luckily, some tourists encountered him and called for medical care. He had lost forty pounds in those five days and 25 percent of his blood volume. After his story became known, his life changed. Because of his choices, he could continue to achieve his goals—not in the same way he'd originally planned, but in a way that works for him.

Today, Aron Ralston continues to climb mountains. He continues his life on his terms. What happened to him that day in that slot canyon didn't define his life because he chose not to let it; he chose to continue, and he chose to be resilient.

After Aron was rescued, the park service went in and retrieved his severed hand and forearm. It took a hydraulic jack and a winch. The limb was then cremated and the ashes given to Aron. Six months later he returned to the scene of the accident and scattered the ashes where, Aron said, "they belong."

Think about the significance of leaving his ashes at the scene of the accident. Was this a show of resilience—a symbol that what happened in the past would remain where it happened? That the ashes were his past and like the phoenix, he'd been reborn? That's how I see it. Aron Ralston's resilient attitude toward a life-changing event propelled him forward, not back.

EXERCISE: Burn Your Past

There are times when you need to put the past behind you. You need to make room in your life for all the good and close the chapter on the pain and hurt.

In this exercise you are going to leave the past behind and, by doing so, clear the path to your future.

Think about someone who is bothering you. Now write a letter to the person who is making you angry. Tell her everything you feel. Tell her how stupid she are, how she hurt you. Lay out everything. Put all your grievances on paper. Use capital letters if you want. Embellish it. Write it in pen, in marker, whatever you need to do to get all the negativity out. Get it all out. When you are through, take the letter and light it on fire. Burn it until it turns into ashes. Now all the negative energy is gone. Take a deep breath and move forward.

Adapting to Change

One thing a farmer knows is how a change in weather must be accounted for when looking at the harvest. You must also learn to adapt to life's ever-changing weather.

Adaptation is defined as making something suitable for a new use or purpose, or modifying it. It means becoming adjusted to new conditions.

Adaptation is inevitable because change is inevitable. With change comes two choices: use it as a springboard for growth, or react. It is always one of those two responses. Changes in life will either fuel your growth or stop your growth. In either case, it's always your choice. Your choice will be growth. Your choice will be to move forward confidently.

Every single person in the world knows pain. We have all experienced it in one way or another. The longer you live, the more experiences you have that help shape and mold your life. If you've had close family members or friends pass away from accidents or medical issues, you have a different perspective than a person who has not had that experience. With each experience you grow, and you adapt to life with your newfound knowledge.

Think of adaptation in your life as though you have just lost eighty pounds. If you choose to keep wearing the same old clothes, they will fall off and you will be embarrassed. When you choose to go and buy smaller clothes, they will fit, and you will look better and feel better. You have adapted to your changing weight, and now you are secure in the fact that you won't lose your pants! In this same way, you can adapt to the changes in your life by "dressing" appropriately and modifying your habits to align with them.

Tamils of the Tundra

Adaptation is a way of life both physically and metaphorically. *Tamils of the Tundra* is an inspiring story of adaptation and choosing to thrive. In the 1990s many Tamil people of Sri Lanka immigrated to Norway. They came from a tropical monsoon climate to a barren land in the Arctic Circle, where the temperature rarely climbs above zero degrees Celsius. Norway had nothing in common with Sri Lanka in terms of climate, language, or customs. The Tamil people had to learn to adapt in order to thrive.

Talk about the challenges of change! The Tamil people could have reacted in any number of negative ways. Certainly this was a situation where a pity party could be in order. But ultimately, the story of the Tamils is a positive one because they chose to see the opportunities in their situation. The Tamil people have learned the Norwegian language, taught their children to ski, and integrated into living in a town of about 2,600 people. In 2002 they numbered 10 percent of the local population. Not only have they integrated, but many also believe they are responsible for the survival of the fishing industry in the small town. By adapting to a totally new place with an open-minded, hardworking attitude, the Tamil have thrived and, in doing so, they have been able to retain their culture and traditions.

This is adaptation. They worked hard to adapt, they worked hard at their jobs, and in the end they were successful.

Learning + Innovation = Success

To innovate is to make changes in something established, especially by introducing new methods, ideas, or products. Innovation can happen in your personal life as well as in your business life.

Innovation demands imagination and using existing knowledge to find a way out of a tough situation. Innovation demands getting out of the box and looking around for a clear picture of the world around you, not just seeing the view from your little box. That's not easy. It takes courage to leave what is familiar and accept the premise that something better might be out there.

There once was a young beautiful princess who had been locked in a tower by a horrible nasty witch. Sounds just like a fairy tale you know, right? Well, it is, but here's the part you don't know. As the beautiful princess looked out the window across the surrounding field, waiting for her prince to come, she thought of nothing more than being rescued. It's too bad she never looked below the window, because, if she had, she would have seen that there was a ladder about six inches below the window and she could have left the tower any time she chose. Now it really doesn't matter whether she didn't know there was a ladder, because her view was only on the surrounding field, or whether she knew about the ladder and was afraid to use it. All that matters is that she remained in the tower until someone came to rescue her. And fortunately for her, someone did come.

For most of you, though, there is no knight on a white horse, no one looking to rescue you from your tower. You have to find your way down. You have to innovate and use your skills to get out of the tower in order to claim your life.

If you feel stuck, look out your window. Look all around. Maybe you can jump, maybe there is a rope, or perhaps you notice a branch nearby. However you have to get out of your situation, find a way. There is always a way. You have to look everywhere and look for merit in every idea. Keep trying until you find your way out.

That is when you find innovation: when you get out of what has become your norm and discover another way and, most importantly, when you act on your discovery.

Starbucks Reinvention

Everyone knows the Starbucks just down the street from where they work. What you might not know is that Starbucks had a few years where they weren't making large profits. They had to find a way to change how they did business. They began with innovative ideas like blonde roast and Via instant coffee. These ideas were in opposition to the original Starbucks idea of freshly brewed, dark roast coffee. Then they expanded more into the area of community involvement and creation of opportunities in the communities Starbucks serves. "I've always said there's not a silver bullet or one single thing that creates a solution," Howard Schultz, CEO of Starbucks, said in an interview. When it comes to innovation, he said, "It's not about being big. It's about behavior." Take the Create Jobs for USA program as an illustration of how new projects get moving at Starbucks: Schultz—still the company's main instigator—has a kernel of an idea (in this case fueled by e-mails he received from customers despondent about the U.S. job market) about how to help create more jobs in communities where Starbucks stores are located. He then activates a team, even inviting members over to his house for pizza, to help create a stir of urgency. Ideas at Starbucks are supposed to undergo a rigorous review process and six to twelve months in the company pipeline. Sometimes, as in the case of blonde roast (eighteen months in development) or Via instant coffee (about twenty years)—it can take far longer. "But we did this in 30 days," Schultz said, pointing to the wristband that is sold for five dollars at Starbucks stores and the website createjobsforusa.org, the money from which is given as capital to small businesses. "I'm going to use this for years as a symbol and example to our people of what's possible."

Between 2007 and 2010, Starbucks struggled to turn their business slump around. During this time there were naysayers who said the Starbucks chain's best days were behind them and they should cut costs on all levels. Starbucks did the opposite. They began to invest in new and innovative ideas. They are even working on a franchise system of healthy drinks. Shultz said, "We have 40-plus years of acquiring real estate and designing and operating stores all over the world. We understand how to elevate and romanticize an experience built around a beverage. And we think we can do that again on a platform of health and wellness, and elevate the nutritious value of what fresh fruit and vegetables can be in a world that is longing for educational tools to eat and live healthier."

Starbucks used its knowledge of the beverage industry and, by adapting to change, they reimagined and innovated the health and wellness industry. They used innovation to discover a new way to succeed and, in the process, ended up doing something more positive than they'd done in the past. Rather than giving in to the struggle, they found a way to turn it around.

Chapter Fourteen

BE HAPPY NOW

Happiness is not something ready-made. It comes from your own actions.

— Dalai Lama —

Life has a way of beating you down, but the choice to stay down remains with you. Don't stay down. Get up, dust yourself off, and get moving. There is always something to enjoy in the present moment. It's finding those small things in the present that keeps you focused on your goals.

The concept you have to understand is that happiness is a choice. You have the power to choose happiness. No one can take that away from you. It's always your choice.

If you want to thrive in life, and not just exist, you must believe you can have anything you want and be willing to work for it. You must focus on the positive and believe that things will get better. In fact, they are great *now* and only getting better.

Have the Muffin

My wife, Andrea, loves to run and as I'm writing this has competed in sixteen marathons. Because she is aware of the many benefits of running, among them the ability to be able to eat what she wants, she started a habit of running a half marathon every Thanksgiving. She does this because she plans to enjoy the Thanksgiving meal, choosing to eat the mashed potatoes, her mother's delicious homemade rolls, the stuffing, and the pumpkin pie. She's aware that eating this without exercising would not be good for her body. Because of her awareness, she runs. This in turn makes her happy. She stays on track with her fitness goals and can eat all the wonderful Thanksgiving treats on the table. It's a win-win situation for her.

There are times in life when you want that red velvet cupcake, and you don't have to deprive yourself of it. Just be aware that when you eat that cupcake, you have to exercise or reduce your calorie intake to balance it out. You should look forward to the cupcake and plan accordingly. You do not have to deprive yourself of things you want, you just need to plan for or work for them. In many cases, you can have what you want and still maintain your goals.

It's the same with finances. You see a couch you want for the house. You know that purchasing the couch will hit you in the pocketbook. It's not that you can't have the couch—you just need to plan for purchasing it. You can do this by cutting down on spending in one area or by working harder, or both, knowing all the while that you can have the couch. Once you are aware of the consequences of buying the couch, you can make plans. Once again, you can have everything.

The whole concept of being happy now is important. While you are working to achieve your goals, you have to enjoy the road to success. As you work, you can have the things you want. You don't have to deprive yourself of everything you want in order to be successful. You need to plan for your goals. When you achieve them, don't feel like you should have done more. My wife, Andrea, eats Thanksgiving dinner without regrets, because she planned to do so. Enjoying all the food was her goal, and she is able to do that because she put in the work with the morning run.

No Regrets

Most of the people I know whom I would call health nuts—the ones who bike every day, or work out at the gym or Crossfit, or run marathons or triathlons—when you ask them why they exercise, there's almost a universal answer. They say that, aside from the endorphins and the positive physical feeling of exercise, they do it because they love to eat. By exercising they can maintain their fitness goals and still eat what they love to eat. Again, a win-win.

When I first started running marathons, a group of us would go on a Saturday training run. We'd get a little hungry because all we'd have were packets of runner's "goo," or energy gels, and we'd start talking about food. I'd always be talking about how much I'd like to eat a pancake and how delicious that would be. One day we started talking about how we'd all like to eat a muffin top like in the Seinfeld episode. Endorphins were high—we were enjoying our run and thinking of our favorite Seinfeld episodes!

Our good friend and trainer Fay Reber hurt his knee and had to stop running at about the eighth mile. Because you plan to run the training courses in advance, you set out water for yourself every three or so miles before you run, so it's waiting for you and you can take a little water break, just like in a marathon. As we arrived at one of our preset points, we saw that Fay had gone to the bakery, bought some muffins and cut the tops off them, and left them for us with a note! We all devoured the muffin tops, and then we continued our training run with no regrets!

There is nothing wrong in having a muffin top when you want one, as long as you plan accordingly. The muffin top I ate that day balanced out with my running. The idea is that you can have everything and anything you want; you just have to plan and work for it. Everything in the world can be yours, if you work for it. You can have everything you want, big and small, when you work for it. You can and should be happy right now. You have good things in your life, right now, and there are more coming to you because you work for them.

There are no shortcuts in life, no secret passages that let you avoid hardships and tough times. You have to keep going, one step at a time. To become the champion you are, you must *Believe It*. You have to believe you can have everything you want, and be willing to work for it.

Working to get what you want will make you happy, because you will see everything you have accomplished. The more you accomplish, the more you believe. Take each and every step on your journey confidently, because you are going to get what you want. You have a destination, you have a path to follow, and you will succeed. When you truly know that, you are already happy.

EXERCISE: What Makes You Happy?

There have been studies on what makes people happy. Here is a list of things that make people happy (find the ones you relate to!):

- Finding money in an old pair of jeans
- Watching the sunset
- Getting into bed with freshly washed sheets
- Learning something new
- Waking up on a sunny day
- Sitting in the sun
- Building sand castles
- Getting a nice message from a loved one
- Cuddling
- Getting a thank-you card in the mail
- Seeing older people holding hands
- Driving a car with the window down on a sunny day
- Watching kids play on a swing set
- Listening to your favorite song
- Being present in the moment
- Listening to upbeat music
- Picnicking in the park or at the lake
- Getting your hands dirty; digging in the dirt
- Making your bed
- Eating seven helpings of fruits and vegetables every day
- Looking back at old photos
- Watching a funny movie
- Getting a quiet moment to yourself
- Walking in the country

- Hearing a baby laugh
- Having a girls' or boys' night out
- Waking up on a Saturday morning and realizing it's the weekend
- Listing three good things that happened today
- Surrounding yourself with happy people
- Fitting into a pair of jeans you thought were too small
- Getting praise from your boss
- Smelling freshly baked bread or cookies
- Taking a warm bubble bath
- Someone telling you that you have lost weight
- Finding out someone likes you
- Playing with puppies
- Smelling freshly cut grass
- Landing at the airport for a vacation or holiday
- Having a good-hair day
- Volunteering
- Hearing someone say, "Thanks"
- Waking up to find out it has snowed overnight
- Smelling rain
- Flying kites
- Spending more time with family and friends
- Going outside
- Helping others
- Practicing smiling
- Being passionate
- Meditating

Entitlement Blocks Happiness

Entitlement comes when a person believes he should have something because he wants it. People with that mentality don't really think much of themselves. You can call it whatever you want, but people who believe they should get everything without working don't have any confidence in their abilities. They expect little from themselves and in doing so, they place no value on themselves.

Many kids learn at an early age, from their parents' actions or lack of action, that they can do or have anything they want without having to earn it. They learn to be disrespectful to their teachers, their elders, and their parents. Because no one holds them accountable for their actions, they feel entitled to have anything and everything they want without working. These spoiled children grow into entitled adults who believe they should have everything. As Jim Morrison of the Doors once said, "We want the world and we want it NOW!" The urge for immediate gratification leads to all kinds of problems: overeating, spending splurges, alcohol and drug use, and disregard for anyone else.

Those thought patterns are never valid for anybody. It is important to believe you can have whatever you want, but don't forget the condition: as long as you are willing to work for it.

This goes back to letting your child break through his or her own egg. Yes, it's painful to watch your child be frustrated and not "make it better." But this is what makes your child stronger, more resilient, and, in the end, successful.

If you are that frustrated child, stop it! No one owes you anything. If you are raising that child, stop it! No one owes her anything. Entitlement blocks success. Entitlement is the weed taking over the bountiful fields you could be cultivating. Get rid of the weeds, and the fields will blossom. Keep the weeds, and eventually all you have is a field of weeds. And there's not much merit or profit in a field of weeds.

No One Owes You a Thing

When Scott was nine years old, his grandparents would come and visit twice a year. Every time they came, Scott was thrilled, because he loved his grandparents and they always brought something special for him. They would praise his accomplishments at school and on the baseball fields. Every visit, his grandfather would carve out time just to spend it with Scott. It was his favorite time of all.

His grandfather would take him out to have a soft drink, and they would have "man talk." His grandfather always said, "The world doesn't owe you a living. You have to make it yourself." This didn't mean much to Scott at nine, ten, or even eleven. But when he was twelve, at their "man talk" he told his grandfather about his terrible teacher and how mean and unfair she was to him. His grandfather listened closely and said, "The world doesn't owe you a living. You have to make it yourself." Scott had no idea what that meant and why this had anything to do with his teacher, but he said nothing to his grandfather.

About three months later, after a particularly hard day at school, he came home and sat alone in his room. He thought about his grandfather and what he'd always told him. Maybe his words did have something to do with his mean old teacher. She didn't owe it to him to be nice. He had to make school as nice as he could for himself. So Scott set about finding ways to make school more fun. His teacher's words and actions didn't seem as mean as before. Scott finished the year, having a pretty good time because he made it so. The next time his grandfather came to visit, Scott couldn't wait for man time. When his grandfather asked him about school, he said, "My teacher didn't owe me a good time. It was up to me to make it." His grandfather smiled and said, "That's my boy."

No one owes you a successful life—not your parents, not your children, not your friends, not your enemies, not your teacher, not the government, not the universe, and not your dog. You alone are responsible for a successful life. If you are sitting around waiting for the world to give it to you, it's going to be a long, fruitless wait.

The Happiness Muscle

The neuroscientist Dr. Richard Davidson has compared happiness to a muscle that can be strengthened with practice. Happiness is a skill that can be learned. You can actually learn to be happier. You know that you can master any skill, and that it just takes time and practice. Remember the 10,000 Hour Rule? You already have a start on perfecting the skill of happiness, because throughout your life you have been happy. You've already been practicing; now's the time to get some serious hours in on mastering the skill of happiness.

Be grateful for your life and your experiences. Everything in life has a negative and a positive. Find the positives, and focus on them. Find the lessons and learn from them. Gratitude for your life will bring you great happiness. When you look for the positive, you may be surprised to find more than you'd imagined.

Be passionate about believing you can have everything you want. Immerse yourself in that belief. Everything you believe has a purpose behind it. Concentrate on where you are going and how you will get there. You know the way, and you know what you want; stay focused on that goal.

As you move forward, you will face challenges, and it's in those challenges that motivation awaits. You will find the solutions, and the solutions will fuel your belief. Happiness comes more often as you practice. You will live each day to the fullest, believing you have a purpose and knowing you are on the path to achieving everything you ever wanted.

Successful athletes have many things in common, one of which is that they are focused on solutions. If they find they need more training, they make it happen. If something isn't working right for them, they find another way. It's the same for you. Focus on the solution to the problem, rather than on the problem itself, and you will find the answer. Lingering on the problem only brings negativity to your life and keeps you stalled in the past. Push past the problem to the solution, to the present, and make things happen. You control your destiny. You alone are in charge of how you live your life, what emotions you choose, and how you achieve your dreams.

Be passionate about what you believe! Look deep inside and discover what it is inside you that inspires you to belief. What makes you want to jump out of bed every morning and get started on your day? What will keep you going when things aren't going the way you want?

Every person has a passion inside. Search for it and when you find it, bring it out and let it light the way for you like a beacon.

You must always focus on the solution to the problem, and not just the problem. By focusing on the solution, you remove yourself from the victim mentality and move toward your goals. Remember, you have the power to control your thoughts and ultimately your destiny.

Remember the joke, "Wherever you go, there you are." You can choose how to see where you are. No matter what your present circumstances are, you can choose how you view it. Regardless of where you are, there is something positive to be found. The adage "When life gives you lemons, make lemonade" illustrates a positive mind-set. No matter where you are or what your situation may be, you have the power to choose how you see it and how you act.

Practice Gratitude

A study by Robert A. Emmons and Michael E. McCullough showed that keeping a gratitude journal of five things the study participants were grateful for, once a week, had a huge impact. They called this "gratitude lite."

They found that the people who kept this short journal, one sentence for each of the five things, were significantly happier after two months and more optimistic than the control group that didn't keep a journal. They also exercised more and had fewer physical problems than the control group.

When the studies included polio survivors and others with neuromuscular problems, they again found that those who kept the gratitude journal were happier and more optimistic. These people also slept more soundly, slept longer, and woke up happier than those in the control group.

"If you want to sleep more soundly, count blessings, not sheep," Dr. Emmons advises in *Thanks!*, his book on gratitude research.

Think Happy, Be Happy

How you view your present circumstances makes a difference in your happiness. When you learn from every experience, you can find a positive. You change your mind-set and focus on what you learned, what you did well, and what you can improve on. By focusing on lessons and solutions, you find the positive and you work out your happiness muscle.

Changing your mind-set is the key. Is the glass half full or half empty for you? It is half full because it half-emptied in the past, and you now live in the present. You believe the glass will again be full, so live as though it is a full glass, because what happened to the half that's gone doesn't really matter.

Show forgiveness to yourself and to those around you. Holding on to a grudge and focusing on the negative will only bring you down, and happiness is hard to find when you are angry. Showing forgiveness is a skill you can learn. To be happy, you can't carry around negativity with you all the time. Yes, things happen in your life, and people do things that hurt or anger you. But if you carry the anger, the anger wins. Once you find forgiveness, anger leaves, and happiness can take its place. You will see everything clearly without the veil of anger clouding everything. Life's too short to stay angry, and you are never in control of your own life when you are angry. Take charge of your life and be happy right now.

The steps to happiness are always the same. You must take every single one of them in order to discover the happiness you deserve, the happiness you require, and the happiness that will give your life meaning every single day. One of the steps may be easier and one more difficult, but you must take every single step.

1. Show gratitude.

2. Be passionate about believing it.

3. Stay focused on the solution, not the problem.

4. View your present circumstances in a positive light.

5. Show forgiveness to yourself and others.

Your happiness depends on you. You choose whether to be happy. Every day will bring you new opportunities. Every day will give you the power to choose how you live your life. Choose to be happy. Practice the skill of happiness. There is every reason in the world for you to have it all. Just *Believe It!*

EXERCISE: Today Is the Day

If you're like most people, you have more to achieve and desire more than you could accomplish in just one more day. So here's your wake-up call: You can have everything you want. You have to believe and work for it. If you want to have a wonderful relationship with your family, work on it today. If you want to be financially independent, work on it today. If you want to live the life of your dreams, work on it today. Start right now.

So, if you work every day on your dreams, are you happy? That's the million-dollar question. What makes you happy? Is it something from outside, or does it come from within you? Can you choose to be happy? Yes.

You need to Be Happy Now. There are many ways to do this, and every one is under your control. Stop for a moment and think about the things you haven't done, the things you might regret not doing later.

What are the five things you would do if this were the last day of your life?

1._____

2._____

3._____

4._____

5._____

Why would you do those things?

1._____

2._____

3._____

4._____

5._____

Why aren't you doing them right now?

1._____

2._____

3._____

4._____

5._____

If you aren't doing the things you would do on the last day of your life, it's a clear sign that your life is out of balance. In the workbook at the end of this book, you'll find an exercise I call the 7 Pillar Self-Assessment. It will help you identify the areas in which you need to take some action to bring balance and happiness back into your life.

Afterword

GET OFF YOUR *A* AND ON TO *B-C-D*

You don't have to be great to start, but you have to start to be great.

— ZIG ZIGLAR —

EVERYBODY KNOWS his or her *ABC*s. *A* is where you start. *A* is where you are. You're born with your A. You are the best, the top, the A." In order to keep that A you must learn the BCDs. As great as an A is, there's not much you can do with one letter. You need to have more letters in your life.

You live your life in the BCDs. Everything you want to accomplish is in the BCDs. With your A you can have more in your life. With the *BCD*s everything becomes possible. Your *A* can move on and join the party. Here's what they stand for:

B is for *Believe It!*

C is for *Create It!*

D is for *DO IT!*

DO IT!—like the old Nike "Just Do It" commercials—is two simple words you can use to live your life. Two simple words to give you everything you ever wanted. Do it, work at it, do it. It's simple. Put in the work and make it happen.

Everything you've read about in this book will help you with your BCDs. Everything you read is another step toward your goals.

You know what you want. Now make a plan to achieve it by looking at your situation realistically and then implementing the plan. It doesn't have to be perfect the first time. You can and should adjust the plan as needed. That's where flexibility comes in. Adapt your plan to the situation as it evolves. Don't get stuck on one thing and let time pass you by. Be flexible and reprioritize as needed. You will be successful.

One of the steps some people struggle with is sticking with what they have now, believing somehow it's going to magically change. Albert Einstein summed it up perfectly: "Insanity is doing the same thing over and over again and expecting different results." Believe Einstein; he was Einstein! He knew his stuff—take this opportunity and learn this truth for yourself.

If something isn't working, it's not going to work tomorrow or the day after. You have to be willing to make changes, and some changes come hard. Change is scary. It's a step into the unknown, and few of us willingly choose to venture into the unknown. We seem to reserve that for *Star Trek* characters and other pioneers or heroes. Now it's time for you to be a hero and a pioneer in your own life. If you don't do it, who will?

THE *BELIEVE IT!* WORKBOOK

Every book is written so that you, the reader, will get something from it. This book is written to inspire you to see yourself as you can be, not as you currently are. You can achieve everything you want in life, but first you must believe that everything is possible. After that you need to work.

You can have it all.

You can have everything you've ever wanted.

You can have everything in life you want, you just have to be willing to work for it, perhaps harder than you have ever worked before. That's what Believe It! is all about. Do the work, have it all.

So now that you've finished the book and hopefully have been priming yourself for change through the exercises in each chapter, it's time to take a step back. Now we are going to put the pieces together so you can create a concrete plan to get out there and accomplish everything and anything you want.

This workbook is about action. It may be looking inside to clarify what you want. It may be coming up with a plan to follow. But everything in this chapter will bring you closer to your goals. Here we go . . .

The 7 Pillar Self-Assessment

Everything in life needs to stay in alignment to work properly. When you are traveling down a road that is fairly straight and flat, your trip is easier. When you drive on a road with hairpin turns and steep hills, the trip is miserable and sometimes you can't even make it to your destination. Roads need to be in alignment so they can be traveled.

So it is with your life. Your life needs to be in alignment. Smooth transitions from one part to another are important so you can live the life of your dreams. When one thing is not in line, then everything in your life suffers. Your life has many different aspects to it, but I've identified seven main parts, what I call the 7 Pillars. The 7 Pillars are the seven primary areas of your life in which you want to make sure you are balanced and aligned with the things most important to you. The 7 Pillars are mental, spiritual, physical, family, financial, career, and social. When properly aligned, they hold your life on a secure foundation. When they are not aligned, your life will tilt one way or the other or completely fall apart.

In this crucial first step, you're going to evaluate where your life is today. Being aware of where you are will help you choose what you want to focus on and what you want to improve. Each of the pillars interacts with the other six and is thus affected by them. For example, if you choose to not focus on your health and become sick, it will impact your family, your career, your financial status, and so on. Every base piece needs the strength of the others to stand strong.

The following graph represents each of the 7 Pillars. Using a scale of one to ten, mark on each row where you think you are right now with regard to how well you are doing or how satisfied you are with each area of your life.

Mental	1	2	3	4	5	6	7	8	9	10
Spiritual	1	2	3	4	5	6	7	8	9	10
Physical	1	2	3	4	5	6	7	8	9	10
Family	1	2	3	4	5	6	7	8	9	10
Financial	1	2	3	4	5	6	7	8	9	10
Career	1	2	3	4	5	6	7	8	9	10
Social	1	2	3	4	5	6	7	8	9	10

Take a look at your graph. Connect the dots. Is the line straight? Where do you need to improve? What are the areas in which you are doing well?

Aligning Your Life

Once you see your life's current alignment, you can make the changes needed. Look for ways you can work on more than one pillar at once. For example, perhaps your score reveals that you need to work on your family and physical pillars. To tackle both of these at once without becoming overwhelmed, you could combine your efforts and:

1. take family hikes

2. play softball, soccer, or tennis with the family

3. go camping as a family

4. join a gym together and go as a family

Another example: You need to work on career and physical pillars. You could improve in both pillars if you combine your efforts and go to bed one hour earlier and get up one hour earlier. Using your newfound morning time, go to the gym first thing in the morning before work. It's been proven that exercising before your day has begun will give you an energy boost and bring more clarity to your work. This new routine will in turn will allow you to get to work earlier and be more productive.

Setting Your Goals

Research data from Dr. Gail Matthews at Dominican University proves the success of goal setting. It's important to understand that setting a goal and doing it correctly will vastly improve the probability of achieving your goal.

In the study Dr. Matthews, a psychology professor, recruited 267 participants from the United States and overseas from a wide variety of groups, businesses, and organizations. The participants were then randomly put into five different groups. Each group was asked to focus on business-related goals they wanted to accomplish in the next four weeks. The groups were divided as follows:

- Group 1 was asked to **think** about their goals.

- Group 2 was asked to **write** their goals.

- Group 3 was asked to **write** their goals and **write action commitments** for each goal.

- Group 4 was asked to **write goals and action commitments** and **share the commitments** with a friend.

- Group 5 was asked to do **everything Group 4 did plus send a weekly progress report** to a friend.

A little more than half the original group, 149 participants, completed the study. At the end of the study the participants were asked to rate the progress and degree of completion of their goals. The results were as follows:

- Group 1 accomplished 43 percent of their goals

- Group 2 accomplished 60 percent of their goals

- Group 3 accomplished 50 percent of their goals

- Group 4 accomplished 64 percent of their goals

- Group 5 accomplished 76 percent of their goals

You can see the clear difference between those who write their goals and those who do not. It is also clear to see that sharing the goals with a friend makes a difference in accomplishing goals. This is what we call the "accountability factor" and is the principle behind many popular goal-oriented programs like Weight Watchers.

Now that you are armed with this information, it's time for you to begin writing down your goals. First, let's brainstorm: Write down everything you dream of being, doing, and having. Don't think about it! Just put a pen to paper and write. Don't stop writing until you have a list of at least twenty ideas. If you have a company or a family, be sure to include them in your goals.

1._____

2._____

3._____

4._____

5._____

6._____

7._____

8._____

9._____

10._____

11._____

12._____

13._____

14._____

15._____

16._____

17._____

18._____

19._____

20._____

Go back and review the ideas you wrote down for ways to get your life back into proper alignment. Can you combine any of those ideas with the goals you've written here? If so, take that step. If not, add three to five "alignment" goals to the list and star them or otherwise mark them so they stand out, because these goals are going to be top priorities in your life. Remember, you must have your life in alignment to give you a solid foundation for everything else, including achieving your bigger goals and dreams.

Now take each goal you wrote down and in one sentence write down why you want to be, do, or have that particular goal. If you cannot define why you want it, then it is not a goal or dream, it is likely something you heard somewhere and thought it would be cool. Believe me, I'm not judging you—I've made this mistake before too. On my first goal list, I had written down that I wanted to hike Mount Everest. When I tried to write down why I wanted to accomplish that in one sentence, I couldn't come up with anything. So I eliminated it from my goals.

Remember what we discussed in Chapter Four: You must know your motivation, or you are unlikely to achieve that goal. It simply won't be a sustainable effort, as you won't have anything to hold on to emotionally when things get difficult.

So, again, next to each goal on your list write down one sentence explaining why you want that goal so badly. This will help you start to narrow down the list.

Next, looking at each of your remaining goals, ask yourself:

1. Can I emotionally commit myself to achieving this goal no matter what?

2. Can I see myself reaching this goal?

3. Is it morally right and fair to everyone concerned?

You must be able to answer *yes* to these three questions. Remember, if one person can accomplish something, so can another.

Now we're going to narrow your focus even further. Categorize your goals into:

- short-range goals (1 month or less)
- intermediate goals (1 month to 1 year)
- long-range goals (1 year or more)

Last but not least, you must be specific with your goals. "Have a nice home" or "be a better parent" or "make more money" is not specific. Revisit your list and break each goal down to details so they are as specific as possible. Here are some examples of specific goals:

- Buy a three-thousand-square-foot modern home with four bedrooms and three baths.
- Spend ten minutes each night with each child listening and spending time with them.
- Earn an extra ten thousand dollars within twelve months

Rewrite your remaining goals and their "whys" in detail, in the appropriate time frame that follows.

Short-Range Goals

GOAL_____

WHY_____

GOAL_____

WHY_____

GOAL_____

WHY_____

GOAL_____

WHY_____

GOAL_____

WHY_____

GOAL_____

WHY_____

GOAL_____

WHY_____

Intermediate Goals

GOAL_____

WHY_____

GOAL_____

WHY_____

GOAL_____

WHY_____

GOAL_____

WHY_____

GOAL_____

WHY_____

GOAL_____

WHY_____

GOAL_____

WHY_____

GOAL_____

WHY_____

Long-Range Goals

GOAL_____

WHY_____

GOAL_____

WHY_____

GOAL_____

WHY_____

GOAL_____

WHY_____

GOAL_____

WHY_____

GOAL_____

WHY_____

GOAL_____

WHY_____

GOAL_____

WHY_____

Out of these goals, choose up to four goals that you need to work on right now. That's right, only four. An important key to success with goal setting is not to overwhelm yourself, or you're unlikely to achieve anything. Personally, I work on two at a time, one short-term goal and one intermediate or long-term goal. As I accomplish one, I replace it with another.

If this is your first goal-setting experience you might want to start with two short-term goals. The confidence you build as you accomplish each goal will enable you to sustain your efforts for longer periods of time, and your odds of achieving your intermediate and long-term goals will go up dramatically.

Goal #1 _____

WHY_____

Goal #2 _____

WHY_____

Goal #3 _____

WHY_____

Goal #4 _____

WHY_____

Last but not least, decide which friend you are going to share your active goals with and how you are going to report to him or her. Then schedule the time for you to work on your goals, ideally with a daily effort. Even it's just ten minutes, taking steps toward your goals every day builds discipline and will ensure that you stay on track. If your goals are important, you will find the time to do it.

Believe It! It *will* happen, because you are working toward it.

Creating an Action Plan

To get what you want, you need to do more than just identify your goals. In the last few pages you decided what you wanted and why. Now you will need to discover the skills and other resources needed to accomplish these goals so you can develop an action plan to achieve what you want.

There are seven steps to reaching a goal. They are always the same.

1. List your goal and your "why."

2. List the benefits of reaching this goal.

3. List obstacles to reaching this goal.

4. List skills required to reach this goal.

5. List people, groups, and companies to work with to reach this goal.

6. Make a plan of action to reach this goal.

7. Set a deadline or completion date.

Let's look at an example so you can understand how these steps work. If your goal is to earn an additional ten thousand dollars in the next twelve months, your plan could look like this:

1. List your goal and your "why."

Earn an additional ten thousand dollars in the next twelve months in order to create a savings cushion. My annual income is $ XXX,XXX.00 (Use your goal income)

2. List the benefits of achieving this goal.

Improve self-image

Sense of accomplishment

Options on how to spend, invest, and enjoy

Reduce worries about emergency situations like job loss or illness

Confidence that I can do it again

3. List obstacles to reaching this goal.

Lack of discipline

Bad habits

Time management

Persistence; stick-to-it-iveness

Low self-confidence

4. List skills required to reach this goal.

Communication

Focus

Creativity

Create good habits

Step out of comfort zone
Positive attitude
Work through the *no*s
How to win friends and influence people

5. List people, groups, and companies to work with to reach this goal.
Family
Financial advisor or mentor
Employer
Direct manager
My church/God
Someone else who has accomplished this goal

6. Make a plan of action to reach this goal.
Make a commitment
Self-discipline—cut TV time
Get an extra job
Start a home-based business
Work on it three hours per day

7. Set a deadline or completion date.
Twelve months from today!

Another example could look like this:

1. List your goal and your "why."
Lose twenty pounds in four months to reduce my risk of heart disease so I can live a longer, healthier life with my family. I weigh XXX and feel amazing! (Use your goal weight)

2. List the benefits of reaching this goal.
My clothes will fit
My blood pressure will be lower
I won't get out of breath walking up the stairs
I can do more things with my family

3. List obstacles to reaching this goal.

Lack of discipline

Cooking for family

Bad habits—late-night snacking

Confidence

4. List skills required to reach this goal.

Create new, good habits

Cook healthy meals

Get moving thirty minutes every day

Drink eight to ten glasses of water every day

Show gratitude every day

5. List people, groups, and companies to work with to reach this goal.

Family

Mentor, Weight Watchers, Jenny Craig

Weight-loss apps

My church support group/God

Someone else who has accomplished this goal

6. Make a plan of action to reach this goal.

Make a commitment

Self-discipline—cut TV time and use it to exercise

Work on it daily

Buy more fruits and vegetables

7. Set a deadline or completion date.

Four months from today!

Now it's your turn. Here's the basic outline; all you need to do is make copies for each goal you are currently working on and then fill it in!

1. **List your goal and your "why."**

2. **List the benefits of reaching this goal.**

3. **List obstacles to reaching this goal.**

4. **List skills required to reach this goal.**

5. **List people, groups, and companies to work with to reach this goal.**

6. **Make a plan of action to reach this goal.**

7. **Set a deadline or completion date.**

Use Affirmations to Stay on Track

When you go to a movie, you know it's not real, yet you will laugh, cry, scream, and react to the movie as though it's real. Similarly, when you imagine that you possess what you want and tell yourself that you already have it, your brain believes it is real and your brain will change. If you take four minutes a day for ninety days, you can reprogram your brain to accept and pursue your goals and dreams even while you are sleeping! Because you choose your affirmations, you choose your thoughts, and you choose the results. Again, your affirmations are real to your brain.

Affirmations are your self-fulfilling prophecy and a daily reminder to stay on the road to accomplishing everything you want. Because your brain sees your affirmations as real, you will begin to see what you believe. When you see something you begin to focus on it and suddenly the opportunities are everywhere.

Financial guru Suze Orman suggests to her viewers that they say, "I have more money than I will ever need." This is one of her own personal affirmations. Oprah Winfrey said on *Larry King Live*, "You really can change your own reality based on the way you think."

In Chapter Five, you experimented with the power of affirmations using a general but powerful self-esteem booster. Now it is time for you to write affirmations that are unique to you, and unique to what you want. You already have a list of what you want to achieve and do right now. Once again, it's critical that you focus on what is most important in your life. For example, if your goal is to make an extra ten thousand dollars in the next twelve months so that you can have a savings cushion, you might use one or more of the following affirmations throughout your day:

1. I am more wealthy than I ever imagined.

2. I am grateful every day for the wealth I have.

3. I earn ninety thousand dollars and live a comfortable life.

If your goal is to lose twenty pounds in four months so you can reduce your risk of heart disease and live a long, healthy life with your family, you might use the following affirmations:

1. I weigh 160 pounds and have a lean healthy body.

2. I love being physically fit and being at my ideal weight.

3. I easily control my weight through exercise and diet.

The following is a list of affirmations, some of which I've used myself, that you can change as you like to make them your own. Or, use them as a creativity boost for writing your own fresh affirmations.

I am the creator of my own reality.
I am the perfect weight for me.
Abundance is available to me always.
I am healthy and strong.
I obtain success in any activity I choose.
I live life to the fullest.
My life is full of joy and happiness.
The more I help people, the more I receive.
I am authentic and present.
I control my thoughts and create my own reality.
I love and respect myself.
I have unlimited potential.
I attract exactly what I need effortlessly.
I have a wonderful partner who loves and trusts me.
I am at peace.
My body heals quickly and effortlessly.
I forgive myself and others.
I can learn more and always have confidence.
I have support from my family in friends.
I have a home overflowing with love and peace.

I only think of positive things and only positive things come into my life.
The doors of opportunity are always open to me and I walk through them effortlessly.
I see the lesson and blessing in everything in my life.
I am successful at everything I do.

For each of your active goals, you will want to write one to three affirmations. What is important to you right now? Be certain you know exactly what your goal is. See it clearly and understand why this goal is important to you.

GOAL: _____

Affirmations

1._____

2._____

3._____

GOAL: _____

Affirmations

1._____

2._____

3._____

Now that you have written some affirmations, it's time for you to get up and walk to the closest mirror. If you don't have your affirmations memorized, take the book with you. When you get to the mirror, look at your reflection and say your affirmations with conviction. This is a way of getting your sense of sight in alignment with your sense of hearing.

Say them out loud. Say them in the present tense. Watch yourself say them. Repeat them until you believe them. Repeat them until they become a mantra for you. Spend at least five minutes every single day saying your affirmations.

When you say your affirmations you have to believe them. As you say your affirmations you *will* believe them. Repeat them until they are a part of you. Until you find yourself saying them without thinking about it.

You have to believe they are true, because they are. Your brain believes they are true, and so you will make choices and act in ways that are consistent with your affirmations.

Feel free to put them to music and sing them. It doesn't matter how you hear them, just as long as you hear them from your own mouth out loud or read them. You *Believe It*.

Start a Gratitude Attitude Journal

Life is about making choices for yourself and having a positive outlook. This isn't always easy, but you can do it. Everyone has things happen in their lives that are not good, things beyond their control. The difference between you and them is that you know how to deal with these times. The number one trait all successful people have in common is a positive attitude.

One of my favorite ways to remain positive each day is to use a gratitude attitude journal. We talked about this a little in Chapter Fourteen as one of the crucial keys to happiness. But writing in a journal daily with a focus on gratitude and maintaining a positive outlook is more than just a happiness tool—it ultimately supports any effort you are making in life, especially those that may pose challenges such as achieving a difficult goal.

Imagine that you have taken on a second job in order to make enough money to build up your savings account. It's going to get exhausting, isn't it? And maybe you will feel resentful some days when your friends or your family go out and do something fun while you're on your way from one job to the other. So how do you keep stepping toward your goal without quitting, and without alienating everyone around you because of your bad attitude? That's right, you focus on staying positive. And we already know that writing down what we want helps us focus on what we want. So in your journal, you start writing about how grateful you are to have found that second job, to have a supportive family who understands that you are trading time with them for a chance to improve your circumstances, and even to be healthy enough to work the hours you are taking on.

Right now, if you haven't already, get yourself a nice notebook or even a fancy journal to write in. Whatever suits you and makes you feel good. Commit to at least five minutes at the end of every day—it's not a lot of time, but it will have an incredible impact on your life. Each evening or night, think about what you are grateful for. Maybe that day a kind stranger paid your toll for you. Maybe your loved one met you for your lunch. Maybe you enjoyed a beautiful sunset on your way home. Whatever it is, write it down. Some days will be easier than others, of course. On the days you don't feel particularly grateful or even happy, focus on listing at least three things, however small, that you are grateful for. You will find that by the end of the exercise, your perspective will have shifted and so will your mood.

Celebrate the Amazing You

You are an amazing person. You can have anything you want because you are willing to work for it. But along the way, it's important that you take care of yourself. This can be as simple as getting a new haircut, taking a long bath, spending an hour reading, taking a long walk, or taking the family on a picnic. Anything you don't usually take the time to do and something that is a treat for you will nourish your spirit and recharge your positive attitude.

What is one thing you can do for yourself that you can afford today?

_____

Why did you choose this? _____

When can you do it? _____

Write the time and day you will do it: _____

Now go and do what you have chosen and celebrate yourself!

Abundance flows to me.

NOTES: _____

_____

_____

_____

_____

_____

_____

_____

_____

_____

_____

_____

_____

I succeed in everything I do.

NOTES: _____

_____

_____

_____

_____

_____

_____

_____

_____

_____

_____

_____

I have endless talents I use every single day.

NOTES: _____

I am successful and wise.

NOTES: _____

_____

_____

_____

_____

_____

_____

_____

_____

_____

_____

_____

_____

I have the perfect life for me.

NOTES: _____

_____

_____

_____

_____

_____

_____

_____

_____

_____

_____

_____

_____

About the Author

RANDY LANG is a self-made millionaire, entrepreneur, and motivational speaker. Randy's dedication to helping others believe in themselves is one of his passions. He strongly believes in giving back, and regularly participates in Ecclesiastical activities. He is actively involved in numerous philanthropic works.

Randy lives in Draper, Utah with his beautiful wife, Andrea, and their three children.